P9-CCV-594

THE ART OF PERSUASION

A *National Review* Rhetoric For Writers

Linda Bridges
&
William F. Rickenbacker

Introduction by William F. Buckley, Jr.

CONTINUUM · NEW YORK

*To those who since the founding have taught and encouraged
NR's writers to cultivate their own stylistic voices whilst caroling
in the choir of the "Lords Spiritual"—especially Jim Burnham,
Willmoore Kendall, Suzanne La Follette, and Mabel Wood, and
very especially Bill and Priscilla Buckley.*

1993

The Continuum Publishing Company
370 Lexington Avenue
New York, NY 10017

Copyright © 1991 by National Review, Inc.

All rights reserved. No portion of this book may be reproduced,
stored in a retrieval system, or transmitted, in any form or by any
means, electronic, mechanical, photocopying, recording, or
otherwise, without the written permission of The Continuum
Publishing Company.

Book design by Michel Design

Printed in the United States of America

Library of Congress Cataloging-in-Publication Data

Bridges, Linda.
    The art of persuasion : a National review rhetoric for writers /
Linda Bridges & William F. Rickenbacker ; introduction by Willam F.
Buckley, Jr.
        p.   cm.
    Includes bibliographical references.
    ISBN 0-8264-0584-3 (pbk. : acid-free)
    1. English language—Rhetoric.   2. Persuasion (Rhetoric)
I. Rickenbacker, William F., 1928–   II. Title.
PE1431.B73   1993
808'.042—dc20   91-67486
                                                                   CIP

AUSTIN COMMUNITY COLLEGE
LEARNING RESOURCES

TABLE OF CONTENTS

Introduction

THE BIOGRAPHICAL NOTE at the end of this book reveals that many years ago a correspondent at the University of Southern California wrote to challenge the construction of a sentence with which I had led off in *Esquire* magazine. Linda Bridges wrote so engrossingly and with such passion and conviction that I came very close to yielding her her point. I didn't, actually, but I made it a point (see Zeugma, below) to look her up on a visit to Los Angeles where I discovered that she was a mere undergraduate. It took me all of fifteen minutes to offer her a job at *National Review*, which offer she accepted but only after advising me that she would first finish her studies in literature. I am not sure I am entitled to say that she has been happy at *National Review* ever since, but I know that I am entitled to say that *National Review* has been happy with her ever since, deferring to her as Managing Editor. She runs a tight syntactical ship, as readers of the magazine will I think acknowledge; but she does so without any sense of oppression, and that is a distinctive aspect of this book, of which she is the co-author. The collaborators know what they are writing about, are serene in their generalities; but if you disagree on any one matter, why, *tant pis*; people have been wrong before, like that guy who wrote that odd sentence in *Esquire* a generation ago.

William F. Rickenbacker ("Dear Wm," he addresses me when he writes, signing off, "Wm," and giving me the opportunity to reply exactly in kind) is a bird of paradise who crossed our path ten years before Linda, when he set out (unsuccessfully) to establish in court that the Census Bureau was exceeding its constitutional authority by sending him to complete the "long form" the Bureau inflicted on one out of one thousand Americans (or whatever the figure was), the Bureau's design being to assemble data of such particularity as to enable the government to come up with a consummate portrait of *Homo americanus*. Wm. wrote for us a spectacularly provocative article at the expense of the Census Bureau—stylish, learned, witty, and so very very wicked as to leave the government absolutely no alternative but to prosecute him for contempt, or else to apologize and close down its offices in an auto-da-fé. He did not go to jail, but he did come to *National Review*, where he served as a Senior Editor until wanderlust set in. It isn't difficult for this to happen to someone so profusely gifted. Wm. could make a living teaching English—or French, or Latin, or Greek, or German, or music (as a critic, or as a performer on the piano), or aviation (his father was Captain Eddie Rickenbacker [BLOCK THAT POLYSYNDETON—see below]. His specialty is total demolition, but his tools are wryness and learning. And, at the receiving end, derelicts tend to go away smiling, except the Bureau of the Census.

This book is sheer enjoyment. I have not read Isaak Walton on fishing, or Whathisname on Melancholy, but that is only because I have zero interest in fishing, and even less in melancholy; but everybody, I think, has an interest in language, and in words, and in usage. And what Bridges and Rickenbacker do here is assemble, more or less as the subjects occurred to them, a few chapters, vehicles for insights and definitions and analysis about language. They give these chapters flippant titles, but they are never thoughtless, and after you finish Chapter Four, for instance, "Kick Up Your Heels" is exactly what you will be glad the chapter impels you to do, as B & R examine the shibboleths of formal writing and show you examples of exactly how a violation of said shibboleths provided the distinctive buoyancy in the references they cite. A word about the references here and elsewhere: they are marvelously chosen, from the composite library of a lifetime's reading by two inveterately curious verbal explorers who have not spent all those years in the stacks without collecting a huge inventory of potsherds. This book would be fun to read even if you blocked out everything written by its authors, so rich are the illustrations.

I wanted to say that, and one other thing in this brief introduction to this volume by my former colleagues, and it is that they frequently wrap up a paragraph's analysis of the use or misuse of this or that rhetorical device with a wonderful grace note. The section on "Hyperbole" gives us a careful, scholarly definition and then begins to wind up. "Hyperbole seems a ready breeding ground for advertising men and political adventurers—reason enough, right there, to avoid it pretty consistently." End there? Oh no! "Nay, squash it with your foot and throw it to the wolves." "Onomatopoeia" is defined, and an example given ("A needless Alexandrine ends the song / That, like a wounded snake, drags its slow length along"). The authors explain: "There is great freedom of invention in this figure. You can screech and howl to your heart's content." I especially like "Periphrasis," which is calmly defined as a roundabout way of talking, and three sentences later you come to the authors' final word on the subject. "Revolution? Nothing of the kind, sir. A few of the boys gathered at Boston Harbor the other evening and had a tea party, in some quantity, for they are lads of high humor, you know, sir, and . . ."

And I for one can't resist writing of that kind, especially on a discipline that is the music of the mind, writing: the art of persuasion. You will count yourself blessed for the experience Miss Bridges and Mr. Rickenbacker have given us.

WFB

Preface

I T IS ASSUMED (yes! that vicious criminal, the passive voice! Take that, Strunk! Put that in your pipe and smoke it, E. B. White! Like it or lump it, Rudy Flesch!)—it is assumed, we say, that you, the reader, already know how to write a clean, lucid, standard, normal, "correct" English sentence. You can spell, you can punctuate, you can parse. You have been taught . . .

> CARPING CRITIC: Another passive! Defend this second crime if you can!

> LB & WFR: Thought you'd never ask. We like the way this passive suggests a large, formless, nameless bureaucracy, a *nomenklatura* of teachers, and the teachers of teachers, and the drudges who write schoolbooks on How to Write.

. . . you have been taught to prefer short words, to avoid the passive voice, to write short sentences, to avoid foreign phrases, to use concrete terms, to avoid expressing opinions, to sit straight in your chair and not play with your food—and, Lo and Behold, it has come to your attention that your sentences all look alike and you are putting your readers to sleep. What? You, *dull?* Your vanity has taken a heavy drubbing. You do not like this one whit. You desire to reform yourself. Congratulations! You have come to the write place.

But, you will ask, can a bright way of writing, an interesting or seductive style, be acquired simply by learning a few tricks from a book? Well, why not? If two generations of Americans have learned to write dull and undistinguished prose by applying a few rules from a book (Use short words! Make short sentences! Avoid foreign phrases! Use concrete terms!), another generation can unlearn those rules and apply better ones.

But, you will ask—and you *are* being touchy, aren't you—in

1

order to write brightly and interestingly, doesn't the writer have to be a bright and interesting person himself? Not at all. Writers aplenty have achieved marketable readability without being major "personalities" in their own right; one thinks of Maugham, Forster, Didion. Wasn't it Garrick who said that Oliver Goldsmith "wrote like an angel, but talk'd like poor Poll"?

Let's illustrate the point with a study of two passages. Here's the first:

> After all these years I can still see that old time just as it was: the town drowsing in the summer morning; the streets almost empty; one or two clerks sitting asleep in front of the Water Street stores, with their splint-bottomed chairs tilted back against the walls, chins on their chests, hats pulled down over their faces; a sow and a litter of pigs going along the sidewalk, picking up watermelon rinds and seeds; two or three little piles of freight scattered about the 'levee'; a pile of 'skids' on the slope to the stone-paved wharf, and the town drunkard asleep in their shadow; two or three wood flats at the head of the wharf, but nobody to listen to the waves lapping against them; the great Mississippi rolling its mile-wide tide along, shining in the sun; the dense forest on the other side; the 'point' above the town, and the 'point' below, cutting off the river-view and turning it into a sort of sea, a very still and brilliant sea.

That is not a bad effort at all. It is the kind of thing a gifted foreigner who had studied English diligently might be able to compass. But the passage lacks personality. It is readable but not memorable; we do not feel any human force behind it. And that is because we have removed from it most of the touches that its author included, and you will agree that this lobotomized version is a far cry from what Mark Twain actually wrote in what is perhaps his most gorgeous work, *Life on the Mississippi*. Here's what happens when a wildly original spirit comes at us, armed with the whole English language and then some, and starts swinging:

After all these years I can picture that old time to myself now, just as it was then: the white town drowsing in the summer's morning; the streets empty, or pretty nearly so; one or two clerks sitting in front of the Water Street stores, with their splint-bottomed chairs tilted back against the walls, chins on breasts, hats slouched over their faces, asleep— with shingle-shavings enough around to show what broke them down; a sow and a litter of pigs loafing along the sidewalk, doing a good business in watermelon rinds and seeds; two or three lonely little freight piles scattered about the 'levee'; a pile of 'skids' on the slope to the stone-paved wharf, and the fragrant town drunkard asleep in the shadow of them; two or three wood flats at the head of the wharf, but nobody to listen to the peaceful lapping of the wavelets against them; the great Mississippi, the majestic, the magnificent Mississippi, rolling its mile-wide tide along, shining in the sun; the dense forest away on the other side; the 'point' above the town, and the 'point' below, bounding the river-glimpse and turning it into a sort of sea, and withal a very still and brilliant and lonely one.

There we see the great old man himself, the melancholy humorist who could spot the mental collapse of store clerks and the business acumen of piglets and the fragrance of drunkards, and who saw on the moving waters of the principal transportation artery of this continent little more than a lonely sea.

The more a writer's personality suffuses his style, the better his style will be. Two centuries ago Buffon put the matter more simply: *Le style est l'homme même.* If God saw fit to fashion you out of the dull and humdrum, still you can heighten and enliven your prose by calling into play the ideas and techniques we offer in this manual. Like as not you do have something to offer in the way of personality but have been timorous, askeert to let fly, and perhaps unsure of the legal speed limits in the English language. Be of stout heart on that score. By the time we have taken you to the outer limits of English prose, you'll be itching for a brawl. Floorboard it, and see what it'll do!

Writing is an art, and much of art is sheer craftsmanship.

The world is filled with pianists who sound very like one another, but the grand panjandrums of the keyboard stamp everything with their own mark. Turn on the radio and listen for a minute (we have had this experience often) and you don't have to be told who it is if it's Alicia de Larrocha or Arthur Rubinstein playing. But there are hundreds of thousands of other pianists, interchangeable pianists, who make decent livings on the strength of their craftsmanship (German: *Kraft*, strength, efficacy). It is no mean goal to shoot for the same in one's writing.

What we offer here is technique for writers, just as Hanon some generations ago spelled out the basic finger exercises for pianists. If you pay attention to the tools we place in your hands, you will free yourself forever from the kind of prose that gives your friends the blind staggers.

Dig in! The whole language and all its strange ways and all its history are yours for the asking. Use them, play the whole keyboard. Who sez you can't write a long sentence when it's already there inside your head? Who sez you can't invent a word if you want to? "River-glimpse"! Who sez you can't say *merci beaucoup?* Write backward and upside down who sez you can't? Trust yourself, trust your reader. If what you say makes sense to you, you will "connect" (E. M. Forster's word). Give your trust, above all, to your words. This means more finger exercises: working that dictionary till it falls apart. Know how strong each word is, know how little support it needs from little you. "Unique," for example, means one of a kind. To write "very unique" is to confess that you don't trust your word to strut its stuff. That sort of attitude hits the reader hard. He figures to himself that if you don't trust your own words, there's little reason for him to trust you. So he becomes a former reader of yours.

Go, and do. And when you publish that best seller, will you send us a note of thanks?

LB & WFR

CHAPTER ONE

Grab Your Reader!

A S A WRITER you have one job alone: to entice your reader to move along to the next sentence. And the job begins with the first sentence of any story, article, chapter, or book. See how some of the masters have handled it:

> In 1937, I began, like Lazarus, the impossible return.[1]

> Chinon still keeps its luck, after all the centuries.[2]

> Born the day after Christmas, 1902, like a wet firecracker, as my mother remarked, I entered a world that lived with and by other creatures.[3]

> In our house on North Congress Street in Jackson, Mississippi, where I was born, the oldest of three children, in 1909, we grew up to the striking of clocks.[4]

> It is trying on liberals in Dilton.[5]

> This is another book about the dissolution of the West.[6]

> *No, here they are . . .* [ellipsis in original].[7]

> The worshipful young gentleman that ruleth over this Society, accosting me some weeks since—it was, if I mistake not, the anniversary day whereon his Majesty and the two Houses of Parliament were delivered from the diabolical Powder Plot— the young gentleman entreated me, in the wantonness of his humor, to attend at this banquet and discourse somewhat thereafter of virtue and good letters.[8]

By prosody I mean behavior, rime's deportment, movement, melody.[9]

Where patriots stood, in the spring of seventy-six, depended upon whether they believed in Original Sin.[10]

My country is the Mississippi Delta, the river country.[11]

The Mississippi Delta begins in the lobby of the Peabody Hotel in Memphis and ends on Catfish Row in Vicksburg.[12]

In each of these opening salvos you see something that looks like a statement but that actually implies and invites a question. What impossible return? How was Chinon lucky? What is it to live "by" other creatures? Why so many clocks sounding off? Why do libs have tough sledding in Dilton? What is "deportment" in rime? What does Original Sin have to do with the question of independence? Who dat on Catfish Row?

The writer has grabbed you by arousing your delight in puzzles and mysteries. That's one way. Another way is to stop short of stating your full case, letting the reader fill in the gaps for himself. If you can hornswoggle the reader into collaborating in your little venture in communication, you have probably hooked him for the duration. Note the sly skewing of signals in the following piece of riot:

> That an act is illegal might conceivably give some shadow of reason why a politician should object to it. The exceptional politician might even, indeed, in an atrabilious moment, object to an act because he found it immoral or dishonest. Objection, however, to an act which is neither illegal nor dishonest, merely because it is *unbecoming*—this represents a distinction which, to put it gently, few politicians of today could be expected to draw under any circumstances. . . .[13]

Understatement in one form or another, whether direct or roundabout, by denying the opposite (of, say, a Croesus—direct: he has enough to get by on; roundabout: he isn't exactly poor), invites the reader, once again, to take part in the proceedings and supply some shade of meaning. Belaboring the obvious either angers or stupefies your reader; giving him credit for a functioning brain not only compliments him but stimulates him in the exercise thereof. And if he feels stimulated when he reads you, guess what? He will think you are a stimulating writer. Bingo!

Mark Twain's daughter Susy died in the bloom of her beauty at the age of twenty-four. As a youngster she secretly began writing a biography of her father, and that innocent effort, with the old man's comments on it, forms a large and poignant part of his memoir. At one point the father comes across this passage in his dead daughter's hand: "Grandma couldn't make papa go to school, so she let him go into a printing-office to learn the trade. He did so, and gradually picked up enough education to enable him to do about as well as those who were more studious in early life." Mark Twain's comment:

> It is noticeable that Susy does not get overheated when she is complimenting me, but maintains a proper judicial and biographical calm.[14]

And if you can read that without cracking at least a little smile, you're tone deaf and you're in the wrong business, pardner. Observe, by the way, that Mark Twain uses both forms of understatement. The direct, "noticeable": *noticeable?* it sticks out like a sore thumb! And the ironic denial, "not overheated," which has the extra merit of being a canny choice of word.

Another way to rope your reader into the festivities is to refrain from all those zealous little "transitions" that writers of how-to-write books love so dearly. We didn't take you by the hand just now and explain where we were going when we shoved off into that paragraph about Susy Clemens, did we? You had just read a paragraph on the virtue of understatement and then you found yourself smack dab in the midst of a paragraph on Susy. Without giving you a transition, we left you to your own devices and trusted you to tag along. At the same time we implied a promise: we were saying you could trust us and all would be made clear by and by. If we kept our promise and wrapped up that general passage with a return to the discussion of understatement, we did our duty, and you had some sense of a confidence not misplaced. If that sort of thing happens time and again, you should begin to trust us as writers, and of course trust is not only the irreplaceable basis of all communication but is also one of the more profound channels of connection between human beings. If you as a writer can make your reader feel that he trusts you to continue in a certain satisfactory way, then you can entice him to read the next sentence and then the next.

You can keep the reader actively collaborating with you by letting him fill in a multitude of small gaps: if he can come up with the information you left out, he feels flattered and happy; if he can't, but you have taken pains to make sure you haven't omitted really vital stuff, no harm's done to your discourse. We didn't identify Croesus, above, but you could nose out from the context that he was a moneybags. We allowed you to figure out, if you didn't already know, that Susy Clemens was . . . etc.

Indeed, it may be that the very essence of an effective style is the sense a reader has, when he falls in with it, that he has somehow become a partner in the proceedings. Poe begins several of his stories in the second person, speaking to the reader straight off. Emerson never strays far from the second person, usually in the form of the imperative, as befits a renegade dominie accustomed to issuing commands:

> Trust thyself: every heart vibrates to that iron string. Accept the place the divine providence has found for you. . . .
> Do not think the youth has no force, because he cannot speak to you or me. Hark! in the next room his voice is sufficiently clear. . . .[15]

And when Emerson, in sudden exuberance of animal spirits, expands the society to include the first person, and speaks of "you and me" and the convivial "we"—well, the poor reader can do little more than thank God he has been invited, all smirched and

unworthy, into such august and toplofty company. He wouldn't
dream of turning his back on the Great Man who has made pals
with him; he will not put that book down.

In classical times it was customary to kick off a big performance with a ritual invocation of the Muse, a gesture Milton
exhumed at the start of *Paradise Lost* (and elsewhere but less
notably). Our own Thoreau laces the first many pages of his clas-
sic, *Walden*, with exhortations and philippics aimed at his fellow
townsmen in Concord. Herman Melville starts one whale of a
novel with the dour command,

> Call me Ishmael. Some years ago—never mind how long
> precisely . . . I thought I would sail about a little. . . . There
> now is your insular city of the Manhattoes. . . . Look at the
> crowds . . . Circumambulate the city. . . . What do you see?
> . . . How then is this? Are the green fields gone? What do
> they here? But look! here come more crowds. . . . Strange!
> Nothing will content them. . . . Once more. Say you are in
> the country. . . . Take almost any path. . . .[16]

And so on, for several pages, and occasionally throughout the
long narration. Is he not a genuine *Orteguiano,* with the reader in
mind at all times?

Note, *en passant,* the rhetorical force of a question or an ex-
clamation ("What do you see? . . . Strange!"). Both invite the
reader to pull a little taffy on the side, making the eye, in Lowell's
fine phrase, "twinkle in furtive connivance."[17]

You were about to ask about *Orteguiano.* This is a follower, a
devotee of the greatest essayist of our age, José Ortega y Gasset.
His *Revolt of the Masses* put his name in bright lights, but he wrote
two dozen other books of equal power and cogency, and
throughout his works he showed a constant interest in matters of
"style." His longest excursion into this territory has to do precisely with the relation between the writer and the reader, and who
could say it better than the man himself?

If the reader analyzes what has pleased him in my work, he

will find that it simply consists in my being present in each paragraph of mine, with the timbre of my voice, and my gesticulations, and he will find that if one puts one's finger on any of my pages, one feels the throb of my heart. But let the reader look deeper and then he will find the true key. That I am present in each expression does not result from any supposed gift of mine, any 'genius' more or less, and even less does it result—this would be indeed repugnant—from my thrusting myself, like Chateaubriand, into my work and forcing the reader to bump into me—it may be observed that I have almost never spoken of myself—, *quite the contrary*: everything proceeds from my *putting the reader* as much as possible into my writings, from my counting on him, trusting him, and making him feel how he is present before me, how he interests me in all his actual, distressed, confused, and errant humanity. It seems to him that there rises from between my lines a hand, ectoplasmic but authentic, which touches him, which wants to caress him—or else, very courteously, give him a good punch.[18]

That is good as far as it goes, but Ortega sidesteps the great paradox of style. Certain it is that a self-indulgent writer who ignores the needs of his reader, cites passages in the original Urdu, crushes ill-sounding words together, pays no attention to rhythm, and breaks the promises that are implicit in the act of communicating—for example, there is implicit in the beginning of a sentence the promise or presumption that the writer will bring it to a conclusion—a promise spectacularly broken by James Joyce, for no useful purpose, at the end of *Ulysses*—certain it is that that writer will be haled before the court for his literary crimes just as surely as Mark Twain brought suit against poor Fenimore Cooper. But it is not true that a writer who obliterates himself, removes from his writing every trace of personal taste or memory or crotchet, and sets down pale perfect sentence after pale perfect sentence, all politely contrived to "involve" the reader, has thereby achieved a "style."

Style—and Ortega knew this—*est l'homme même*. But it is

less a man's philosophy than his fingerprints. Style does not hammer away at you, page after page, with obtrusive opinion. What Ortega was talking about was not so much style as readability, amiability. Style, *l'homme*, comes across in a variety of different ways: in the choice of words, in the boldness of syntax, in the originality of phrasing. Ortega, like Shakespeare, was a highly gifted inventor of words, and some of his coinages (e.g., *vivencia*) have passed into the language of the learned if not that of the campesino. So it is that the most readable of modern essayists is also in style the most individual: put your finger on a page of his, as he says, and there you feel his heart throbbing. And yet the paradox is that he himself has placed the *reader* first in his mind!

There is no doubt that Ortega contained within him the knowledge of this paradox. On the question of style he left us in no doubt:

> To write well consists in constantly making little erosions in the grammar, in the established usage, in the reigning norm of the language. It is an act of permanent rebellion against the social environs, an act of subversion. To write well implies a certain radical boldness.[19]

> Style is the deformation of the common tongue for the special purposes of the speaker.[20]

So he knew. He knew the signal value and charm of treating the reader courteously and decently, consulting the reader's needs and imaginings, allowing the reader to step forth and take a role in the drama unfolding. All this involved his suppressing or mitigating his more eccentric and capricious literary paraphernalia, the scarcely communicable private languages we pick up, like cockleburs, as we go grazing through life: baby talk, lovers' secret lingo, the arcana of professional moguls. And yet he knew also that some considerable degree of license and play must be accorded to the writer if he is to put his stamp on his work, if he is to exist in his work and by existing become a target of interested inquiry. So there are "erosions" and "rebellions" and "deformations" running along below the surface of courtesy and altruism.

Few writers have managed this business of steady assault upon "normal language" better than Albert Jay Nock. Here is a representative page from his golden little variant on the genre of autobiography:

> The war of 1914 ended in an orgy of looting, as any rational being might have known it would, even if he had never heard of the secret treaties which predetermined this ending. It ended as all wars have ended and must end. Any pretence to the contrary is mere idleness. One can say for Brennus that he was no hypocrite, exuding repulsive slaver about 'mandates,' 'reparations,' and the like. He chucked his sword on the scales, saying *Vae victis*, and that was that. Of all the predatory crew assembled at Versailles, the only one for whom I had a grain of respect was old Clemenceau. He was a robber and a brigand, but he never pretended to be anything else, and he was a robber in the grand style. His attitude towards his associates pleased me. He regarded Lloyd George, Wilson, Orlando and their attendant small-fry from a lofty height of disdain, as one might imagine Jesse James or Dick Turpin regarding a gang of confidence men, area sneaks, porch-climbers. He also took no pains to disguise his opinion of them, which delighted me. If you left your watch and pocket-book at home, you could do business with Clemenceau. He would not poison your rum-and-water or besmear your character, and all his cards were on the table. As highwaymen go, one has a good bit of respect for that sort.[21]

"Orgy of looting" is a pretty colorful way to describe the Versailles conference. The rest of that sentence and the next two sentences amount to the flat-footed assertions of a man confident in his ability to reach conclusions and comfortable in his association with you the reader: it is a sort of bassackward way of showing trust. The abrupt leap to classical allusion (Brennus) is an example of something we have already been through; the unexplained allusion is itself a compliment to the reader, as is the untranslated Latin snippet. "Slaver," a harsh substitute for drivel, lets us know we're dealing with a gent who calls a spade a spade and who doesn't stick at using words normally banned from front parlors. This old boy has been around, that's what we begin to see. "Chucked" is even more colloquial, or so it seems nowadays, but Nock would surely have known that it was in use and in print as early as the sixteenth century. "Robber" and "brigand" come at us from our blind side, a nicely calculated little surprise by way of explaining why Nock had "a grain of respect" for the thieving old Frogue. And who would think of saying a robber was "in the grand style"? Now comes "small-fry," a touch of the colloquial to clear the air, followed by the correct and sedate "lofty height of disdain," followed by admiring references to highwaymen and thugs English and American.

By lacing his sentences with this constant flow of breezy, earthy, seemingly vernacular verbiage, Nock succeeds in relaxing our guard. We are almost willing to forget his legendary erudition in a multitude of disciplines ancient and modern, and concede that he is, after all, a decent chap, a good fellow to chat with for an hour or so, over a beer or two, at a café somewhere in northern Europe. He disarms us.

Variety in diction is something we discuss in more detail later on. The point here is that a writer gains the acceptance of the reader by using—on occasion—the lower reaches of diction, by showing he's one of the guys. In a society daily growing more populist and demagogick, this is no niggling achievement. One has built a bridge.

CHAPTER TWO

Hold Your Reader

ONCE YOU have your reader's attention, how do you keep it? Anyone who reads newspapers, reports, news magazines, trade journals will recognize the sensation: you are reading along, your eye traversing the sentences smoothly, only to have the brain wake up three paragraphs later and wonder what it has just been told.

The remedy is not a matter of set formulas of sentence structure and word choice. As we saw from the Mark Twain passage in the Preface, the trick is largely observation: observing the actual details of the scene you wish to describe (or of the economic or political argument you wish to make), then finding analogies to other fields, and finally noticing whether the language you have used suggests more than you consciously intended; if so, either suppress it or hone it, depending on what your subconscious was up to.

John McPhee has the reputation of being one of the great observers of our time. Does he deserve it?

> Foresters, in the main, welcomed the state's new policy [of allowing citizens to cut their own wood], because it would publicize forestry and the forests, but they worried also about the inherent risks. A glimpse of a city person working the woods with a chain saw was enough to make a forester avert his eyes. It would be the forester's job, after all, to sort out felled limbs, seeing which had twigs and which had fingers. Felling and cutting trees was dangerous work for professionals, let alone amateurs. Workmen's-compensation

rates for the logging industry were as high as for any industry in the country, and the timberlands were full of
thumbless pros who seemed to be suffering from permanent
concussions. Minimally, any woodcutter coming to the state
woods needed a hard hat, hard shoes, and a knowledge of
felling techniques. But they came instead in suède and
sneakers, untutored, bareheaded. Most apparently were un-
aware, too, that the preponderance of trees that the foresters
had marked for cutting were alive and standing—good
green timber, which would be ready to blaze across the
hearth and ease the energy crisis by the Fourth of July. Green
wood will burn, after a fashion, but it deposits droplets of
creosote inside the chimney, and the deposits build up until
they themselves catch fire. Then flames lick the roof and start
back down through the building toward the fireplace.[1]

The passage is chock full of details, some the products of direct
observation, others of research: the workmen's-comp rates, the
proper and improper headgear and footgear, the tendencies of
green wood. But McPhee lifts himself out of the category of mere
camera eye with the line about different sorts of felled limbs—in
which verbal conceit and physical image are almost inseparable—
and the one about flames starting back down toward the fireplace,
an understatement more powerful than any dire warning about
the dangers of unskillfully laid fires.

This is where the raw material of observation links up with
the elements taught in composition classes: types of sentences
(simple, compound, complex, compound–complex—and don't
despise the fragment), levels of diction (standard, highfalutin, colloquial, specialized), types of figurative speech (metaphor, simile,
synecdoche, et al.), external reference (quotation, allusion). The
key is variety, though remember that you want to lead your
reader on, not trip him up: you want to keep him guessing what
is coming next, not make him give it up and turn to something
more enticing, like maybe Arthur Schlesinger's cyclical theory.

Here is a passage that takes unvaried sentence structure and
heavy repetition and rides them out the window:

In the late winter of that year it was very cold (*cero absoluto*) and we were quartered in the barracks of the Insulation Works near Poughkeepsie and made sorties into the surrounding areas to insulate the great *villas* and split-levels along the river, with Rinaldo, my driver, handling the great truck (*automóvil monstruoso*) and me handling the heavy insulation gun with great dignity and much technical confusion; and in the day it was very fine and clear and cold, but in the night just cold—in fact, freezing (*congealo el rumpo*), because the unspeakable gas company had shut off the unspellable heat in the unpronounceable barracks.

In the morning the orderlies would come through and bear away the bodies of those who had frozen during the night, so that the politicians became angry and issued three pair of thermal underwear to each man and insisted that all three pair be worn at once, which was a great indignity and an obscenity, considering the technicality of the zippers and the back-flaps, so that at last the men began to wear the back-flaps *décolletés*, for emergencies, which is a difficult thing and technical, and still there were many sad events.[2]

If the and and ands, and the unspeakable unspellable unpronounceables, and the difficult things and technical were not clearly intended as humor, they'd be funny nonetheless; but instead of accounting S. L. Varnado a skillful parodist, we'd be saying he was an over-the-hill novelist.

Here is a passage that does what Varnado deliberately did not do:

. . . seeing [Scott-King] cross the quadrangle to the chapel steps, middle-aged, shabby, unhonored and unknown, his round and learned face puckered against the wind, you would have said: 'There goes a man who has missed all the compensations of life—and knows it.' But that is because you do not yet know Scott-King; no voluptuary surfeited by conquest, no colossus of the drama bruised and rent by doting adolescents, not Alexander, nor Talleyrand, was more blasé than Scott-King. He was an adult, an intellectual, a classical scholar, almost a poet; he was travel-worn in the large periphery of his own mind, jaded with accumulated experience of his imagination. He was older, it might have been written, than the rocks on which he sat; older, anyway, than his stall in chapel; he had died many times, had Scott-King, had dived deep, had trafficked for strange webs with Eastern merchants. And all this had been but the sound of lyres and flutes to him. Thus musing, he left the chapel and went to his class-room, where for the first hours he had the lowest set.[3]

Waugh changes his tone and frame of reference almost every clause—sometimes even within a clause. The leisurely sympathy of the first clause, followed by the brisk, contemptuous pity of the second; the "colossus of the drama" (Oedipus? Bacchus? James Dean?); the straightforward Alexander and the devious Talleyrand; the Paterine flights twice followed by the deflating details of Scott-King's daily life.

Now, most of us—even the ones who write for a living—will never write a novel, and it might look odd to start paraphrasing Pater's essay on the *Mona Lisa* in a memo on vacation policy, or even in a letter to the editor of *The New Criterion*. A bank clerk named Leonard Bast wrestles with this problem:

> Leonard was trying to form his style on Ruskin: he understood him to be the greatest master of English Prose. He read forward steadily, occasionally making a few notes.
>
> 'Let us consider a little each of these characters in succession, and first (for of the shafts enough has been said already), what is very peculiar to this church—its luminousness.'
>
> Was there anything to be learnt from this fine sentence? Could he adapt it to the needs of daily life? Could he introduce it, with modifications, when he next wrote a letter to his brother, the lay reader? For example—
>
> 'Let us consider a little each of these characters in succession, and first (for of the absence of ventilation enough has been said already), what is very peculiar to this flat—its obscurity.'
>
> Something told him that the modifications would not do; and that something, had he known it, was the spirit of

English Prose. 'My flat is dark as well as stuffy.' Those were
the words for him.[4]

Every day's mail brings *National Review* at least one manuscript or
letter to the editor from someone who is consciously imitating Bill
Buckley, or Tom Wolfe, or (though usually at one or more
removes) H. L. Mencken. Mimicry has its place, but those who
are not talented don't do it very well, and those who are should
usually be writing in their own voices instead. Throughout this
book we recommend reading as a way to improve one's own
writing. But the improvement comes from learning what sorts of
possibilities are open, broadening our range of knowledge and
vicarious experience. Imitation may be the sincerest form of flat-
tery; it is not usually the best way to communicate.

In later chapters we shall be saying more about the uses to
which various tools can be put; for now we should start by heft-
ing some of them and seeing how they work. First, the different
sorts of sentences.

In the classroom, sentences are classified according to
whether they use conjoined clauses of theoretically equal weight
(compound), subordinated clauses (complex), both (compound–
complex), or neither (simple). But probably no experienced
writer—certainly no editor we have ever met—actually says: I
have (he has) just written three complex sentences; better go back
and make one of them compound. He is more likely to say: Hmm,
that's monotonous—and anyway the first point is more important than the second. In the Waugh example, the first three sentences are all technically compound but very different from one
another in feel. The clause "he was an adult, an intellectual, a
classical scholar, almost a poet"—only one adjective, and that
descriptive rather than evocative—gives the reader respite from
all those prepositional phrases and emotive verbs.

Whether the writer consciously notices them or not, there
are three factors in his decisions on how to shape a sentence:

rhythm, logic, and emphasis. For most thoughts, there isn't one single, necessary rhythm; a warning that the Redcoats are coming, on the one hand, or a description of a lazy summer day, on the other, demands a more or less urgent phrasing. But for most declarative statements, there will be three or four good ways of arranging the sentences—though the different versions won't mean exactly the same thing.

Suppose that Varnado had not been writing a parody, but simply telling a story. He might have written:

> It was very cold that winter, and insulation was in great demand in the large houses along the Hudson. We were based in Poughkeepsie, and every day we went out to work, with Rinaldo driving the truck and me handling the insulation gun.
>
> In the daytime it was cold, but fine and clear; at night, it was just cold—in fact, freezing. Making matters worse, the gas company had shut off the heat in the barracks.
>
> In the morning, the orderlies would come through and bear away the bodies of those who had frozen during the night. Eventually the politicians became angry; they issued three pair of thermal underwear to each man and insisted that all three pair be worn at once. Now, this was a great indignity, since the zippers and back-flaps were hard to unfasten. At last the men began to wear the back-flaps undone, but there were still sad accidents.

Or suppose that he had been drafting the beginning of a complaint to the local newspaper about the stupidity of politicians:

> Insulation was in great demand that winter, since it was exceptionally cold. From our base in Poughkeepsie, we ventured out every day to insulate the large houses along the Hudson; Rinaldo drove the truck, and I handled the insulation gun.
>
> The days were not bad, but at night it was freezing—and to make matters worse, the gas company had shut off the heat in the barracks.
>
> Some men actually froze to death in the early days,

and each morning the orderlies would come through and bear away the bodies. When the politicians learned about this they became angry and issued three pair of thermal underwear to each man; furthermore, they insisted that all three pair be worn at once.

This solved one problem but led to another. Because the zippers and back-flaps were difficult to manage, there were many indignities. Wearing the back-flaps undone was only a partial remedy.

The first version keeps the narrative flow of the original but breaks up the rhythm, so that the reader isn't rocked to laughter. The second is anxious to direct the reader's attention, to point up contrasts and causations.

This is where considerations of rhythm merge into those of logic. In a narrative, the logic will be mainly chronological, but once we get into expository or argumentative writing, we may want to show the relation between different events or thoughts— or we may want to let the reader figure it out for himself. That is one basis on which the writer decides when to use subordinate clauses.

Another is emphasis. Normally, more important statements will be made in independent clauses, with others subordinated in clauses beginning with *when, because, since, although,* and so forth. A reviewer may mention that, in Mrs. Sunstreaked's memoir, her first husband, Mr. Gotrocks, was disposed of in a subordinate clause. Like most devices this can be turned upside down, as in James Burnham's occasional opener, "When I was a Trotskyist . . . ." But more usually (otherwise understatement would not have the effect it does), emphasis grows from suspense, or is left exposed by a sudden reversal. We see the first in a passage on the end of the Tridentine Mass:

What is troublesome is the difficulty one has in dogging one's own spiritual pursuits in the random cacophony. Really, the new liturgists should have offered training in yogi or whatever else Mother Church in her resourcefulness might baptize as a distinctively Catholic means by which we might tune off the Fascistic static of the contemporary mass, during which one is either attempting to sing, totally neglecting the prayers at the foot of the altar which suddenly we are told are irrelevant; or attempting to read the missal at one's own syncopated pace, which we must now do athwart the obtrusive rhythm of the priest or the commentator; or attempting to meditate on this or the other prayer or sentiment or analysis in the ordinary or in the proper of the mass, only to find that such meditation is sheer outlawry, which stands in the way of the liturgical calisthenics devised by the central coach, who apparently judges it an act of neglect if the churchgoer is permitted more than two minutes and forty-six seconds without being made to stand if he was kneeling, or kneel if he was standing, or sit—or sing—or chant—or *anything* if perchance he was praying, from which anarchism he must at all costs be rescued: 'LET US NOW RECITE THE INTROIT PRAYER,' says the commentator, to which exhortation I find myself aching to reply in that 'loud and clear and reverential voice' the manual for lectors prescribes: 'LET US NOT!'[5]

The second device, sudden reversal, is used in this scene in which a young man wakes up the morning after the night before:

> Dixon was alive again. Consciousness was upon him before he could get out of the way; not for him the slow, gracious wandering from the halls of sleep, but a summary, forcible ejection. He lay sprawled, too wicked to move, spewed up like a broken spider crab on the tarry shingle of the morning. The light did him harm, but not as much as looking at things did; he resolved, having done it once, never to move his eyeballs again. A dusty thudding in his head made the scene before him beat like a pulse. . . . During the night, too, he'd somehow been on a cross-country run and then been expertly beaten up by secret police. He felt bad.[6]

If Kingsley Amis, writing his first novel, was tempted to preface "He felt bad" with "In short" or "To sum up" or some other such seeing-eye phrase, the spirit of English Prose stopped him in time.

We saw some wild and woolly shifts in levels of diction in Nock's dissection of the Versailles Treaty in Chapter One. Often, the shifts will not be that extreme.

> It will be generally admitted that Beethoven's Fifth Symphony is the most sublime noise that has ever penetrated into the ear of man. All sorts and conditions are satisfied by it. Whether you are like Mrs. Munt, and tap surreptitiously when the tunes come—of course, not so as to disturb the others; or like Helen, who can see heroes and shipwrecks in the music's flood; or like Margaret, who can only see the music; or like Tibby, who is profoundly versed in counterpoint, and holds the full score open on his knee; or like their cousin, Fräulein Mosebach, who remembers all the time that Beethoven is "echt Deutsch"; or like Fräulein Mosebach's young man, who can remember nothing but Fräulein Mosebach: in any case, the passion of your life becomes more vivid, and you are bound to admit that such a noise is cheap at two shillings.[7]

"It will be generally admitted" is the throat-clearing beginning of the editorial writer. Both "sublime" and "noise" are entirely within the standard level of diction, but *sublime* is a word belonging to heightened emotional contexts and advertising copy, and *noise*, as a musicological term, is more usually applied to Jimi Hendrix or John Cage than to Beethoven. "All sorts and conditions," even if we don't recognize it as coming from the old Prayer Book, is clearly not an everyday phrase. Except for "echt Deutsch" the prose flows along quite normally from then on (logically, by the way, the narrator should have said, "who can *see only* the music"; but poetic license is not reserved for versemakers: it can be issued to anyone with a good enough ear), until it soars once more, like the music, with "the passion of your life"—only to come smiling back to earth with "cheap at two shillings."

In certain elevated contexts, shifts in levels of diction might be inappropriate, but the writer can still avoid monotony through a flexible rhythm:

. . . we have stood at the parting of the ways of the two most vigorous systems of law that the modern world has seen, the French and the English. Not about what may seem the weightier matters of jurisprudence do these sisters quarrel, but about 'mere matters of procedure,' as some would call them, the one adopting the canonical inquest of witnesses, the other retaining, developing, transmuting the old *enquête du pays*. But the fate of two national laws lies here. Which country made the wiser choice no Frenchman and no Englishman can impartially say: no one should be judge in his own cause. But of this there can be no doubt, that it was for the good of the whole world that one race stood apart from its neighbours, turned away its eyes at an early time from the fascinating pages of the *Corpus Iuris*, and, more Roman than the Romanists, made the grand experiment of a new formulary system. Nor can we part with this age without thinking once more of the permanence of its work. Those few men who were gathered at Westminster round Pateshull and Raleigh and Bracton were penning writs that would run in the name of kingless commonwealths on the other shore of the Atlantic Ocean; they were making right and wrong for us and for our children.[8]

This passage—the peroration of Pollock & Maitland's great work on *The History of English Law Before the Time of Edward I*—contains one quotation and one play on a quotation; it has some inversions and some alliteration; but its musical effects come mainly from an alternation between multisyllabic, predominantly Latinate words and short, homegrown English ones.

Of course, there is much more to word choice than level of diction. English has many near synonyms, and many other words that are synonyms in one or more of their senses. Level of diction will play a part in choosing which one to use; so will euphony (of which, more later). Without going as far as Flaubert, who made a fetish of the *mot juste*, we can say that in many contexts one word will be slightly better than all the other possible choices. The only practical way to get acquainted with the alternatives is spending time with the word books—using a dictionary to check that the word you have settled on means what you thought it meant; using a dictionary or a thesaurus, whichever suits you, to find other words that mean nearly the same thing and might be closer to the mark.

A former columnist of *National Review*'s habitually took this too far—and not far enough. This man—a well known writer, as it happens—sometimes used words very oddly indeed. He was hard to reach by phone to ask for clarification, and puzzling out what he might mean was like doing a crossword puzzle in a foreign language. Finally one of the staff noticed that if you looked up the word he had used, and scurried past all the normal near synonyms until you came to a word that was a synonym in only one very restricted sense, chances were you would have found the word he really meant. No examples, we are relieved to find, made it into the printed pages of the magazine, but this was the sort of thing he did: "His ideas found their natural seat in *The New Yorker*"; "This was a heed of disrespect"; "He was not a frank agent."* This is not a common affliction; but, particularly with abstract words, some writers achieve a similar effect by never using the dictionary at all.

A related problem is what Fowler calls Elegant Variation; Kilpatrick's Rule explains how to avoid it: "If you have to refer to bananas four times, use the word banana four times. Don't use three bananas and one elongated yellow fruit."† Elegant Variation is especially common among economics writers. Four stocks respectively rise, skyrocket, edge upwards, and rise; or they fall, plummet, drop, and fall. If Kilpo were giving his advice today, it might have gone: one banana, one elongated yellow fruit, one brightly colored curvilinear *musa*, and one banana.

But we do not have to choose between the Scylla of Elegant

Home, *mark*, and *free*, respectively.

† James Jackson Kilpatrick, whose book *The Writer's Art* (see our bibliographical note, pp. 113-114) gives a more extended form of the same advice.

Variation and the Charybdis of quadruple repetition. Nouns, as Fowler drily remarks, can be replaced by pronouns; verbs in a series can be elided. GNP rose 10 per cent in 1980, 5 per cent in 1982, 7 per cent in 1989, and 2 per cent in 1990. Bananas are grown in tropical regions; they are easy to ship and popular among consumers—especially in banana cream pie. Four thoughts, and only two *bananas*.

A more public-spirited reason to use the dictionary regularly is to stop good words from getting lost. The only language that doesn't change is a dead one. Even Latin, as still spoken in the Vatican, has to acquire new words for new objects and concepts. The French Academy can huff and puff all it likes about *franglais*; if Frenchmen find that *le weekend* expresses their time to spend in the countryside better than *la fin de semaine*, they will say *le weekend*.

But that does not mean writers should not go to some lengths to preserve useful shades of meaning—stopping short of being so pure that no one understands them. *Comprise*, for example, is commonly used to mean its inverse, *compose*, as in "Our Republic is *comprised* of fifty states." But its actual meaning ("to include, comprehensively," as in "Our Republic *comprises* fifty states") is worth preserving, since a) no other single word means precisely that, b) it is not quite dead, and in any case c) using it correctly will not cause misunderstanding. *Protagonist* is still widely used, as it should be, to mean "chief actor," even if some writers think it means simply any character ("one of the minor protagonists in *Macbeth*"), and others think it means "proponent." But *specious*, which until not so long ago meant "superficially fair, just, correct," with the possibility that the fair show was misleading, has come to mean simply "deceptively attractive"; the possibility has become a certainty. To try to revive the older meaning would itself be misleading.

Finally, that subspecies, specialized language, a/k/a jargon. All businesses and pleasures have their terms of art, economical ways of saying complicated things, which are also passwords for initiates. No one at *National Review* would begrudge the computer operator his verb *access*: *gain access to* is cumbersome, and *enter* means something different to the keyboarder. The accountant and the stockbroker need to know what is on the *bottom line*. Some of these words are intrinsically ill formed; others are not (see the comments on *anthimeria*, pp. 86–87). But in either case, when they get out of the corral and start galloping all over the editorial pages, we should reach for our lassos. As Pope put it:

> In words, as fashions, the same rule will hold;
> Alike fantastic, if too new, or old:
> Be not the first by whom the new are tried,
> Nor yet the last to lay the old aside.[9]

Mr. Button-Down may *incent* his sales force in private, if he likes, but in public he should *motivate* it. His increased expenses may *impact* his net earnings, but we hope the revised tax laws won't *harm* his daughter Jennifer's chances of going to a good college.

Bill Buckley once said of Murray Rothbard that there was not really much chance that he would succeed in getting the lighthouses privatized; but at least if he could keep the big-government types arguing against free-market lighthouses, it would be more difficult for them to nationalize the steel mills. By the same token, if we are arguing (as Fowler and A. P. Herbert did) about whether you can legitimately say "under the circumstances" or whether—since *circum* means "around"—it must be "*in* the circumstances," we won't be inclined to say that something will "impact the bottom line."

There are many reasons to use the devices of quotation and allusion: appeal to authority (as one might quote James Madison on the Constitution or Ted Williams on hitting), corroboration (this person, whom you may have heard of, agrees with me), a feeling that there is no need to reinvent the wheel ("What oft was thought, but ne'er so well expressed"[10]). In any case, quotations and allusions broaden the frame of reference: for the reader who recognizes a particular line, it brings with it the memory of its whole context; even the reader who does not recognize it will get a whiff of its history if he is told it was uttered by, say, Winston Churchill.

The method of using quotations is straightforward enough: the writer should give as much or as little of the context as suits his purpose, and quote as short or as long a bit as he needs. How frequently to quote is a matter on which opinions differ. Some writers carry the appeal to authority so far that they seem never to speak for themselves: even if an argument could have been presented as well in their own words, they find a quotation instead. And some readers feel that a writer who sprinkles his work too liberally with quotable quotes is showing off. Certainly one should be cautious about following the advice of an old highschool Latin textbook: "Nothing adds spice to conversation like the use of apt quotations. In memorizing the following Latin phrases, try to picture a conversational situation where each might be fittingly used. Then watch for such an occasion and when it arises use the quotation. Just think of the various occasions where you could appropriately quote: 'Dux femina facti' or 'O terque quaterque beati!' "[11] Just think!

Allusion requires more tact than straight quotation does: the writer must weigh the likelihood that his readers will recognize the allusion against the likelihood that they will be annoyed if they do not. The smaller the audience, the greater your freedom: if you are writing a paper for the C. S. Lewis Society, you can toss in quotations from Lewis without attribution, secure in the knowledge that most of the audience will recognize them, and that those who don't will not resent them. In writing for a more general audience, the allusion should be handled in such a way that it makes sense—even if it lacks its full resonance—to the reader who is unfamiliar with it. The passage from *Scott-King's Modern Europe* sails close to the wind: most educated English readers of Waugh's own generation would recognize the Pater reference; many American readers, and readers of later generations, would not. The Varnado passage, like any parody, depends on the reader's having at least a passing acquaintance with the original; but nearly every American old enough to be reading *National Review* would have run across Hemingway at some point. In the two Forster passages, the Ruskin quotation demands no prior knowledge—everything relevant is contained within the passage—and the phrase "all sorts and conditions" carries its hint of elevation in the words themselves.

We will offer a more technical discussion of the different forms of figurative speech in Chapter Five, but we would like to suggest here some of their appropriate (and inappropriate) uses. Like quotation and allusion, figurative speech—metaphor, simile, synecdoche, and so on—broadens the frame of reference. Its use can be merely explanatory—as when one compares the behavior of the average price level to a seesaw or an elevator, according as one is or is not a Keynesian—or merely decorative, but it is often some of both, as in these images for "Old Western man":

> And here comes the rub. I myself belong far more to that Old Western order than to yours. I am going to claim that this, which in one way is a disqualification for my task, is yet in another a qualification. The disqualification is obvious. You don't want to be lectured on Neanderthal Man by a Neanderthaler, still less on dinosaurs by a dinosaur. And yet, is that the whole story? If a live dinosaur dragged its slow length into the laboratory, would we not all look back as we fled? What a chance to know at last how it really moved and looked and smelled and what noises it made! And if the Neanderthaler could talk, then, though his lecturing technique might leave much to be desired, should we not almost certainly learn from him some things about him which the best modern anthropologist could never have told us? He would tell us without knowing he was telling. . . . It is my settled conviction that in order to read Old Western literature aright you must suspend most of the responses and unlearn most of the

habits you have acquired in reading modern literature. And because this is the judgement of a native, I claim that, even if the defence of my conviction is weak, the fact of my conviction is a historical *datum* to which you should give full weight. That way, where I fail as a critic, I may yet be useful as a specimen. I would even dare to go further. Speaking not only for myself but for all other Old Western men whom you may meet, I would say, use your specimens while you can. There are not going to be many more dinosaurs.[12]

The comparisons here are startling, and then, as we think of them, both delightful and illuminating.

Memory as eyesight ("the mind's eye") is a conventional image; a master hand can deepen it, without carrying it so far as to be comical:

I . . . tried to do something about the amnesic defects of the original—blank spots, blurry areas, domains of dimness. I discovered that sometimes, by means of intense concentration, the neutral smudge might be forced to come into beautiful focus so that the sudden view could be identified, and the anonymous servant named.[13]

There is a need for caution. Figurative speech is one of the greatest sources of humor—intentional (more of this in Chapter Four) and unintentional. Here is a metaphor (unpublished) that got away: "The wave of war babies, having vented their frustration at the establishment, crashed upon the shore of a tightening labor market." The author had noticed that "wave" was a metaphor and sought to elaborate it, but he had not taken the next step and visualized the result. If he had *seen* the bizarre image of a sheaf of babies rising in an arc with the surf, he would have stopped right there and not compounded the problem by throwing in a tightening labor market—a dead metaphor until it becomes the shore, which is apparently also a giant trampoline or firemen's net, being pulled into an ever narrower circle as the unfortunate babies draw nearer. (The extra metaphor of *venting* stays mercifully dead.)

A different writer's also unpublished problem was not the clash of two metaphors, where mere visualization would have sent up a warning signal, but the piling up of nearly synonymous clichés, topped off triumphantly with yet another clichéd metaphor: "When it comes down to the 'nitty-gritty,' 'all cards on the table,' 'chips down,' and 'backs to the wall,' only the two superpowers—the United States and the Soviet Union—have the power to send themselves—and everybody else—'to hell in a handbasket.'" No analysis, we think, needed.

CHAPTER THREE

A Pleasing Style

S TYLE IS the craft, the craftiness, of literature. It is no substitute for genius, which works in the deeper strata of consciousness and unconsciousness. One easily calls to mind any number of writers who have produced works that may endure but whom very few critics hold up as stylists to be emulated: Walter Scott, James Fenimore Cooper, Theodore Dreiser, Charles Dickens, Walt Whitman. These are writers who traffic in mood, emotion, landscape, narrative zing, comedy, peculiarity, suspense, bathos, thrills, and not a few axes to grind. Such work, performed with panache, can often carry the day. After all, isn't it a pleasure to see a genius in action? But genius finds its own way and is not our concern; rather we limit ourselves to the more lowly domain of the pleasing style. What makes it tick?

First, a pleasing style avoids whatever is displeasing. We have discussed the importance of variety in all aspects of style but have not mentioned the basic pleasure that comes from words that sound good together thanks to their harmony and rhythm. It is easy enough to point out the usual traps: clusters of long words elbowing each other off the page, colonies of long words with similar endings (the concatenation of terminations in "-ation" is an abomination), unpronounceable little thickets of look-alikes ("most past post-war recessions"), festering and incestuous love-nests of prepositions ("later on over in Alice's house"), impacted consonants ("Albrecht's strudel"). As for rhythm, in prose if it is noticeable it is objectionable (recall the Safire-Agnew "nattering nabobs of negativism"—and it was not only the three n's that caused the problem but also the tin-eared pounding on that triplet dum-didi dum-didi dum-didi).

Really, all that can be said about melodious and rhythmic writing can be boiled down to this: read aloud what you have written, and if it "lies trippingly on the tongue," you are all right. Experienced stylists will speak a sentence to themselves, run over it in their mind, before they even begin to write it. That saves time. And a fine trick towards achieving a smooth style is to put what you want to say into words of one syllable, at least in your mind before you write the sentence, so that you find the natural rhythm of the language that will be the framework for your completed sentence. It is impossible to write a bad English sentence in words of one syllable; syntax and grammar may be awry, but the words somehow all by themselves have got the hang of it. Listen to the pure speech of the uneducated (the source of the *castizo*, the authentic, as Ortega y Gasset said) and you will have it. A splendid example floated over the broadcast waves not long ago. A New York cop was being interviewed about a burglary. He allowed as how "we apprehended the individual." That is the speech of the half-educated. If he had never seen the inside of a schoolhouse, he would have said, "We caught the man." Give heed, all ye sinners!

Here we may permit ourselves an aside on the matter of obscenity, blasphemy, pornography, skatology, and their sister arts. It is by no means certain that everyone finds these shenanigans pleasing; indeed, it's a lead-pipe cinch that a large part of your readership finds all this low rant disgusting. You don't have to be a bluenose or a member of Watch & Ward to steer clear of this stuff in your own writing, because there are good grounds both stylistic and artistic for doing so. Of course, if you intend to hang out your shingle as a junk dealer, all bets are called.

This business of sounding out a sentence to yourself before you write it to make sure that when you write it the thing comes out straight and lies good on the page suggests something not often thought about: writing is actually one of the performing arts. The performance is at one remove, granted, but the writer's performance exists in time and his reader's understanding of that performance occurs also in time, like music, like the dance. The writer should think of himself as a musician in a recording studio: he will give his performance in what amounts to solitude, but with the knowledge that he will be heard from start to finish by whoever cares to attend, later, at his disembodied but genuine work, as it exists on the printed page. That this is a performing art is shown by the pleasure that writers and audiences alike take when a writer mounts upon the boards and gives "readings"— would not "recitals" be the more accurate word?—from his own works. Poets, from Homer on down (way down) to the present, have troubadoured about and earned a hunk of bread and a sip of wine and mayhap the hand of fair maiden by singing their songs. Charles Dickens picked up a pretty penny in the American boondocks reciting various tearjerk passages from his collected effusions. None other than T. S. Eliot took the time to make recordings of himself reciting his own verses, and a haunting sound it is, that voice part Midwest part New England part Old England coming through grey monotone uttering enormous visions. Our own Robert Frost when he finally had it made kept body and soul thegither by roaming around mainly from college to college chanting his chansons—"barding about," he called it.

We have discussed variety in all aspects of writing, including of course variety in the length of your sentences. It's time to zero in on sentence length in relation to this business of the writer as performer, because clearly your "Jack hits the ball" type of sentence doesn't pass muster as a performance, good or bad. Short sentences made of unremarkable words fitted together in accord with the standard instructions allow the writer no room for maneuver. But let's take a look at a master minstrel as he entertains his audience:

> There stands the city of Bangor, fifty miles up the Penobscot, at the head of navigation for vessels of the largest class, the principal lumber depot on this continent, with a population of twelve thousand, like a star on the edge of night, still hewing at the forests of which it is built, already overflowing with the luxuries and refinement of Europe, and sending its vessels to Spain, to England, and to the West Indies for its groceries,—and yet only a few axemen have gone 'up river,' into the howling wilderness which feeds it.[1]

The great virtue of variety in sentence length is that it invites us to disport ourselves—and, haply, amuse the reader—in truly long sentences that announce themselves as performances. By the time Thoreau has mentioned Bangor and begun to embroil it in his oratory, modifying it first with an adverbial phrase, then a prepositional phrase, then a noun in apposition, and on to a simile and three participial phrases, is there any doubt that he has dropped one shoe, if not a seven-league boot, and is teasing you in the suspense as he *suspends* the second shoe before letting it crash? And doesn't the crash sound fine?

It's fine because you have been party to a performance, a piece of derring-do contrived for your delight. Thoreau has crafted this sentence so that the elements have a certain shape: after Penobscot, the phrases grow shorter and shorter, until the "star" phrase with its scanty twenty-five letters making eight words, and then the phrases grow longer and longer again, the serial "and" makes its appearance, introducing the longest phrase of all, and then the highly theatrical exit-line brings the performance to a rousing conclusion. That "howling wilderness," by the way, was no new stroke: Oliver Cromwell, His Highness the Lord Protector, in his speech in Parliament in the Painted Chamber, on Tuesday, September 12, 1654, had expressed pity concerning the emigration of "those poor and afflicted people . . . into a vast howling wildernesse in New England."*

---

*And perhaps both knew "the waste howling wilderness" of Deuteronomy 32:10.

The sentence, you see, has a shape, in this case the shape of an hourglass. Our definition of a "long sentence" is precisely this, that it must have a shape, a form, a frame, an intelligible structure. It must possess its own length as the necessary condition of its existence, just as a human being possesses his own body and can do no other. This criterion bars the gate to almost every piece of sheer babble and rant, all shopping lists and inventories, all magical incantations (magic is not the domain of intelligibility in structure), all experimental crimes against form (let us have no thrill killers, no Leopold & Loebs of logic), all political orations and similar embarrassments. In all those jungles and swamps of verbiage we do not find the sort of thing that can please a reader, we do not find shapely utterance.

The last thirty pages of that crossword puzzle by the late Mr. Joyce, *Ulysses*, for example, contain no punctuation, but that failing does not elevate the slaver to the august rank of An English Sentence. It is simply a concatenation of short statements interrupted by exclamations. Mr. Fowler is not fooled by this bizarrerie. He classifies, for example, the following—

You commanded & I obeyed

—as "two sentences (not one)." He would classify the Joyce cadenza as a series of sentences or fragments of same, and also as a humdrum example of Celtic tavern-rant. We note that Fowler uses the British terminology, in which a compound sentence is one with a compound subject or predicate; whereas in the American terminology we have used elsewhere, Fowler's example qualifies as compound. But be that as it may, anyone who says the final chapter of *Ulysses* is a sentence that runs on for thirty pages is speaking as a typographer, not a writer.

The ability to expand a sentence is companion to the ability to think, and that in turn comes along by and by with the passage of years, one fondly hopes. A study made some five decades ago shows that the average sentence of a child in the fourth grade ran some 11 words, of a child in the sixth grade 12 words, in the eighth 15 words, in sophomore highschool 18 words, in senior highschool 20 words, in freshman college 20 words, in upperclassman college 22 words. Since then, the iron doctrines of the Strunk-White-Flesch-Bernstein conglomerate have probably served to reduce the average length of sentence in each of the age groups, but it is certain that we could still find sentences growing longer in the elbow as their writers grow longer in the leg. The trouble is that no one has encouraged the young writer to spread his wings and fly into those spacious realms where unlikely things make lovely connections, old memories dance with this afternoon's rainfall, yesterday's weeping melds into love or rainbows or a mess of pottage. "Jack hits the ball" sentences can't handle that sort of thing.

So, in the interest of gaining some variety in sentence length, let's concentrate on what it is that makes a good long sentence (other than a capital crime).

Thoreau's sentence about Bangor exhibits all the basic devices of a good long sentence. If you wish to embark on such a voyage, give a signal to the reader that this is going to be A Performance; let him know when he has reached the halfway point; blow a whistle when the curtain is about to come down; and be jolly well sure that you walk off stage with a good exit-line.

This sounds easy, but none other than Nathaniel Hawthorne made mincemeat of a grand sprawling sentence, the opening shot of *The Scarlet Letter*, and we'll let you look at it and think about it before we obtrude our 'umble judgment:

> In my native town of Salem, at the head of what, half a century ago, in the days of Old King Derby, was a bustling wharf,—but which is now burdened with decayed wooden warehouses, and exhibits few or no symptoms of commercial life; except, perhaps, a bark or brig, half-way down its melancholy length, discharging hides; or, nearer at hand, a

Nova Scotia schooner, pitching out her cargo of firewood,—
at the head, I say, of this dilapidated wharf, which the tide
often overflows, and along which, at the base and in the rear
of the row of buildings, the track of many languid years is
seen in a border of unthrifty grass,—here, with a view from
its front windows adown this not very enlivening prospect,
and thence across the harbor, stands a spacious edifice of
brick.[2]

Do you get the feeling that something has misfired in that
sentence? Hawthorne has put us through some 170 words of
description without giving us a hint of the grammatical subject
and predicate, saving these two most basic elements of the sentence for the final phrase, where, in the strongest position, he
comes up with nothing more interesting than this: "here stands a
spacious edifice of brick."

The contrast couldn't be more vivid than this between Hawthorne, who builds up a tremendous suspense in order to say
next to nothing, and Thoreau, who comes right out with his subject and predicate in the very opening of his sentence—"There
stands the city of Bangor"—and then goes on to construct a sentence that rises phrase by phrase to a stunning climax.

Nevertheless, Hawthorne tried. He adhered to the few rules
of the road for long sentences: he betrayed his intentions early, he
gave the standard signal at the midpoint ("at the head, I say, . . ."),
and he announced the impending conclusion ("here . . ."). All
would have been well if he had only had something to say when
all eyes were upon him. (In his defense one may point out that
brick, being far more expensive than the local building material,
which was the howling wilderness, symbolized wealth and
power in most New England towns.)

These examples from Thoreau and Hawthorne represent
two types of structure: the early appearance of subject and predicate, and the greatly delayed appearance of one or both of them.
We call these The Flying Start and The Dramatic Entrance. The rest

are The Saga, Planned Chaos, and The Four-Masted Schooner, all of which we'll discuss in due time.

The Flying Start

The Flying Start may be the most difficult structure to bring off, because you tip your hand at the outset: the reader is given the subject and the predicate right off the bat, and you face the arduous labor of holding his interest with ancillary details and syntactically secondary phrases. You have given up the syntactical weapon of suspense and must make do with other tricks. We've seen Thoreau. Herewith, three or four good examples from the last century and a half, starting with Bancroft in 1859:

> The wanderers, as they passed along, gazed on trees astonishingly high, some riven from the top by lightning; the pine; the cypress; the sweet gum; the slender, gracefully tall palmetto; the humbler herbaceous palm, with its green chaplet of crenated leaves; the majestic magnolia, glittering in the light; live oaks of such growth, that now that they are vanishing under the axe, men hardly believe the tales of their greatness; multitudes of birds of untold varieties; and quadrupeds of many kinds, among them the opossum, then noted as having a pocket in its belly to house its young; the bear; more than one kind of deer; the panther, which was mistaken for the lion; but they found no rich town, nor a high hill, nor gold.[3]

That effort seems almost disqualified on grounds of being a mere shopping list or inventory until we notice that the structure is nicely set up to express the contrast between the wealth of nature, which the explorers disdained, and the glister of gold, which they sought in vain. The sentence is actually compound: "The wanderers . . . gazed on" at the start, followed by the long inventory, then "but they found no . . . gold." The structure is simple and strong; and it works.

Keynes was a far better rhetorician than economist—otherwise his celebrated and wrongheaded *General Theory* wouldn't have made so much clatter. He was also a pretty sound thinker, even a conservative, in his early days, as witness this salvo:

> It is evident that Germany's pre-war capacity to pay an annual foreign tribute has not been unaffected by the almost total loss of her colonies, her overseas connections, her mercantile marine, and her foreign properties, by the cession of ten per cent of her territory and population, of one-third of her coal and of three-quarters of her iron ore, by two million casualties amongst men in the prime of life, by the starvation of her people for four years, by the burden of a vast war debt, by the depreciation of her currency to less than one-seventh its former value, by the disruption of her allies and their territories, by Revolution at home and Bolshevism on her borders, and by all the unmeasured ruin in strength and hope of four years of all-swallowing war and final defeat.[4]

Here again a stupendous inventory is presented in phrases of various length, culminating in the longest phrase of all (a normal rhetorical requirement), and the question is whether this sentence should be disqualified. We think not. It is composed not so much of syntactical elements as of a rhetorical trick: the severe understatement of the main clause ("capacity . . . has not been unaffected") followed by a bill of particulars, a list of grievances if you will, that obliterates the understatement and brings the reader by degrees to recognize that Germany's capacity has not merely been diminished but has been completely demolished. In order to achieve this effect Keynes must fit the whole bill of particulars into one sentence; the length of the sentence is required by the shape of the utterance. It passes muster.

Another way to organize a Flying Start sentence is to drape it over a framework that exists in the physical world. Will Percy, perhaps the best of our second-rank poets, was, like most poets, a fine worker in prose. Here he takes us on a cruise down the Mississippi:

> Between the fairy willows of the banks or the green slopes of

the levees it moves unhurried and unpausing; building islands one year to eat them the next; gnawing the bank on one shore till the levee caves in and another must be built farther back, then veering wantonly and attacking with equal savagery the opposite bank; in spring, high and loud against the tops of the quaking levees; in summer, deep and silent in its own tawny bed; bearing eternally the waste and sewage of the continent to the cleansing wide-glittering Gulf.[5]

This is quite a different river from the subject of Will Percy's excellent sonnet, which ends with a noble couplet:

Imperial indolence is thine, and pleasure
Of hot, long listlessness and moody course.

This river, instead, is throbbing with activity, which Percy catches in a gusher of participles: "unhurried . . . unpausing; building . . . gnawing . . . veering . . . attacking . . ." He breaks this string with two nicely matched adjectival phrases and then announces the homestretch by returning to the participle ("bearing"). The sentence comes to an end when the river comes to its own end, in the waters of the Gulf. The matter has dictated the form.

This form of sentence is well adapted to summations. Syntactical suspense would actually work to the disadvantage of the writer, whose main concern in a summary is to state his points clearly and get them across with the least distraction; a reader who doesn't know whither the sentence is going may expend some of his brain waves on syntax, the pleasures thereof, while gliding lightly over the underlying mass. Joe Sobran once polished off a review of a book by Garry Wills this way:

For when one comes out of the spell, potent but not lasting, that Wills has cast; when one's ears have ceased to tingle with his resounding codas, it dawns on one not only that apocalypse is not at hand, but even that this turbulent world is a little stabler than one had thought; that though blacks and whites continue to harass and annoy each other, there will be no 'second civil war'; that though Nixon may look pretty silly to those who surpass him in erudition and hipness (in what Hamlet satirically calls catching the tune of the time), still, American society is not quite 'coming apart at the seams'; that though the Catholic Church may seem insufferably backward to the Berrigans' tiny communion of chic saints, yet the gates of Hell will not—not this season, anyhow—prevail against it; and that many things, though tediously obvious, are still true, and need to be insisted on with what Wills once termed 'a Johnsonian humor, reason, and human balance.'[6]

Sobran announces the launching of a major sentence with his two subordinate clauses, gives us The Flying Start, and then sets forth on the inventory of hope that Wills ignores. The beginning of the end is announced ever so quietly with the "and" after the final semicolon, introducing the swiftest clause of all. Whether by design one knows not, but Sobran has rounded his performance with the name of Wills in the first and last breaths of the sentence. Is the sentence a success?

Much the same sort of thing happens in a fascinating sentence that appears in John Cheever's last novel, where we meet a character named Chicken:

Chicken began to cry then or seemed to cry, to weep or seemed to weep, until they heard the sound of a grown man weeping, an old man who slept on a charred mattress, whose life savings in tattoos had faded to a tracery of ash, whose crotch hair was sparse and gray, whose flesh hung slack on his bones, whose only trespass on life was a flat guitar and a remembered and pitiful air of 'I don't know where it is, Sir, but I'll find it, Sir,' and whose name was known nowhere, nowhere in the far reaches of the earth or in the far reaches of his memory, where, when he talked to himself, he talked to himself as Chicken Number Two.[7]

As a final exam for this section of the course, we'll let you have the pleasure of picking out the details of this sentence on your own. Don't fail to read the sentence aloud: Cheever preeminently wrote for the ear.

Do you begin to see the long utterance as some kind of theatrical performance? That's what it is; it belongs on stage. This is why we so seldom find genuine examples of such sentences in an informal setting, such as personal correspondence or memoranda or private diaries. Just as it is bad manners to strut and orate and carry on in a small social gathering, so it is bad manners to fire off twenty-one-gun salutes in a simple personal letter. Your best letter-writers, indeed, have mastered the lackadaisical and all but spineless sentence whose syntax serves the minimal purpose of identifying subject and predicate, a sentence that can run on forever, for all anyone may care, its only responsibility being to mimic faithfully the voice of its author.

As we have mentioned, most writers about the business of writing have contented themselves with outlawing the long sentence, although some of the more literary, such as F. L. Lucas, do recognize that a well made long sentence has a certain dignity. Richard Weaver considered the matter systematically, though only in a footnote:

> Some correlation appears to exist between the mentality of an era and the average length of sentence in use. The seventeenth century, the most introspective, philosophical, and 'revolutionary' era of English history, wrote the longest sentence in English literature. The next era, broadly recognized as the eighteenth century, swung in the opposite direction, with a shorter and much more modelled or contrived sentence. The nineteenth century, again turned a little solemn and introspective, wrote a somewhat long and loose one. Now comes the twentieth century with its journalism and its syncopated tempo, to write the shortest sentence of all.[8]

Here Weaver is painting in swift strokes with a broad brush, and it would be captious to argue details. On the whole he is right, of course; but the twentieth century is fading fast—and good riddance, let us all agree—leaving the prospect that the twenty-first will face more perplexing and thrilling problems, which will require longer and more complicated sentences for their expression. The whole question cries out for study. The time is past when one could simply say, Write short. The time is coming when we shall need to write long.

The Dramatic Entrance

No dramatist puts his principal characters in Act I, Scene 1. Rather, "the stage is set" in one way or another. Minor figures talk about the major figure who is about to appear; some history of this figure arises from the trivial action; and at some tense moment the major character makes The Dramatic Entrance. When it comes to drama and its mating with the English sentence, who surpasses Shakespeare?

> This royal throne of kings, this sceptred isle,
> This earth of majesty, this seat of Mars,
> This other Eden, demi-paradise,
> This fortress built by Nature for herself
> Against infection and the hand of war,
> This happy breed of men, this little world,
> This precious stone set in the silver sea,
> Which serves it in the office of a wall
> Or as a moat defensive to a house
> Against the envy of less happier lands,
> This blessed plot, this earth, this realm, this England,
> This nurse, this teeming womb of royal kings,
> Fear'd by their breed and famous by their birth,
> Renownéd for their deeds as far from home,
> For Christian service and true chivalry,
> As is the sepulchre in stubborn Jewry
> Of the world's ransom, blessed Mary's Son:
> This land of such dear souls, this dear dear land,
> Dear for her reputation through the world,
> Is now leas'd out, I die pronouncing it,
> Like to a tenement or pelting farm.[9]

The grammatical subject of the sentence ("throne" plus a host of nouns in apposition, with their qualifiers) occupies fully 90 per cent of the wordage, after which we get the predicate. This is, *verbo strictu,* the negation of the dramatic entrance: instead of the arrival of the mighty, we have the mighty brought low. But the rhetorical force and form are the same.

In Hawthorne's rambling utterance about the tumbledown wharf in Salem we noted that the conclusion was pretty slim pickings after all that preamble. Shakespeare makes much the same point in one of his few remarks on rhetoric:

> *Iago.* She that was ever fair and never proud,
>   Had tongue at will and yet was never loud,
> Never lack'd gold and yet went never gay,
> Fled from her wish and yet said, 'Now I may';
> She that, being anger'd, her revenge being nigh,
> Bade her wrong stay and her displeasure fly;
> She that in wisdom never was so frail
> To change the cod's head for the salmon's tail;
> She that could think and ne'er disclose her mind,
> See suitors following and not look behind,
> She was a wight, if ever such wight were,—
> *Desdemona.* To do what?
> *Iago.* To suckle fools and chronicle small beer.
> *Desdemona.* O most lame and impotent conclusion![10]

Richard Weaver said the seventeenth century wrote the longest sentence in English literature, but the sixteenth was no slouch. Sir Philip Sidney, a contemporary of Shakespeare, availed himself of The Dramatic Entrance to sum up his arguments in favor of poets and poetry:

> Since, then, poetry is of all human learnings the most an-
> cient, and of most fatherly antiquity, as from whence other
> learnings have taken their beginnings; since it is so universal
> that no learned nation doth despise it, nor barbarous nation
> is without it; since both Roman and Greek gave such divine
> names unto it, the one of prophesying, the other of making,
> and that indeed that name of making is fit for him, consider-
> ing that where all other arts retain themselves within their
> subject, and receive, as it were, their being from it, the poet
> only bringeth his stuff, and doth not learn a conceit out of a

matter, but maketh matter for a conceit; since neither his description nor his end containeth any evil, the thing described cannot be evil; since his effects be so good as to teach goodness, and delight the learners of it; since therein (namely in moral doctrine, the chief of all knowledges) he doth not only far surpass the historian, but, for instructing, is well nigh comparable to the philosopher and, for moving, leaveth him behind him; since the Holy Scripture (wherein there is no uncleanness) hath whole parts in it poetical, and that even Our Saviour Christ vouchsafed to use the flowers of it; since all his kinds are not only in their united forms but in their severed dissections fully commendable; I think, and think I think rightly, the laurel crown appointed for triumphant captains doth worthily, of all other learnings, honor the poet's triumph.[11]

That is a good example of rhetoric in the service of suasion, argumentation. An attack on the poetical movement of the time had been published, and our hero rose in defense. In summarizing his arguments he needed more than a stale rehash; he needed the persuasive power of grand rhetoric. He attained his goal, even though in the excitement of the chase he stumbled into an amphibology (the series of clauses beginning with "since" all modify the main verb, "think," with one exception: the clause in the middle, "since neither his description nor his end containeth any evil, the thing described cannot be evil," which requires "since" to modify "cannot," and therefore maroons the sentence, for sentence it is, in a sea of clauses belonging to "think").

Will Percy needed a long sentence to get a purchase on the great river; Samuel Sewall in 1697 used a long sentence to describe not space, but time, indeed Eternity, as newly seen after the death of the first wave of Puritans:

As long as Plum Island shall faithfully keep the Commanded Post; Notwithstanding the hectoring winds and hard Blows of the proud and boisterous Ocean; As long as any Salmon, or Sturgeon shall swim in the streams of the Merrimack; or any Perch or Pickeril in Crane Pond; As long as the Sea Fowl shall know the Time of their Coming, and not neglect seasonally to visit the Places of their Acquaintance; As long as Cattel shall be fed with the Grass growing in the meadows, which do humbly bow themselves before Turkie Hill; As long as any sheep shall walk upon Old Town Hills, and shall from thence pleasantly look down upon the Parker River, and the fruitful Marishes lying beneath; As long as any free and harmless Doves shall find a White Oak or other Tree within the Township to perch, or feed, or build a careless Nest upon; and shall voluntarily present themselves to perform the office of Gleaners after Barley-Harvest; As long as Nature shall not grow old and dote; but shall constantly remember to give the rows of Indian Corn their education by pairs; So long shall Christians be born there; and being first made meet, shall from thence be Translated to be made partakers of the Inheritance of the Saints of Light.[12]

Sewall by witchcraft takes us from Plum Island, the lovely barrier reef at the mouth of the Merrimack that protects the harbor at Newburyport, all the way to the Saints of Light, giving us an early example of the sprawling syntax that our writers felt so natural and right when talking about the spaciousness and plenty of the New World. That hag Predestination was dead; we would all go to Heaven now; American optimism was aborning. You will have noted that Sewall keeps the structure perfectly clear through his use of coordinated conjunctions ("As . . . As . . . As . . . So"). The final thunderclap of rhyme and rhythm ("Trans*la*ted to be *made* Par*tak*ers . . ." etc.) drives the point home for good.

In the first two decades of this century Paul Elmer More published the eleven volumes of the Shelburne Essays, the most distinguished work of criticism in our literature. Of course he understood the virtues of a spacious architecture in prose and relied on long sentences to summarize great intellectual trends:

When I consider the part played by Stoic and Epicurean philosophies in the Renaissance and the transcendent influence of Cicero's dissertations upon the men of that day; when I consider that the impulse of Deism in the eighteenth century, as seen in Shaftesbury and his successors, was at bottom little more than a revival of this same Stoicism, as it had been subdued to the emotions by Cicero and mixed with Epicureanism; that Shaftesbury was, in fact, despite his worship of Epictetus, almost a pure Ciceronian; and when I consider that out of Deism sprang the dominant religion and social philosophy of our present world—when I consider these and many other facts, I question whether Cicero, while he certainly represents what is more enduring, has not been also, actually and personally, as dynamic an influence in civilisation as St. Paul, though the noise, no doubt, and the tumult have been around the latter.[13]

Here we are given a double signal that the conclusion is nigh. First is the normal serial sequence ("x . . . x . . . x . . . and x"). Then there's a second signal ("x . . . and many other facts"), which announces the wrap-up. Joe Sobran used much the same phrase in the same way ("that . . . that . . . that . . . and that many things"), closing off his review of the Wills book.

The same subject that Paul Elmer More was discussing receives almost identical treatment at the hands of a great poet, writing in prose for the moment:

By destroying traditional social habits of the people, by dissolving their natural collective consciousness into individual constituents, by licensing the opinions of the most foolish, by substituting instruction for education, by encouraging cleverness rather than wisdom, the upstart rather than the qualified, by fostering a notion of *getting on* to which the alternative is a hopeless apathy, Liberalism can prepare the way for that which is its own negation: the artificial, mechanised or brutalised control which is a desperate remedy for its chaos.[14]

Here T. S. Eliot has paid attention to the nice calculation and ordering of the different lengths of phrase, producing something like the hourglass shape we saw in Thoreau's hymn to the city of Bangor. There are two signals that the end approaches: the last item in the list of "by" phrases is the only one that includes a whole subordinate clause within itself; and of course the appearance of the grammatical subject and verb in normal dress tells us the fuse is getting short.

Another poet of ours, writing at about the same time, in a profoundly conservative vein, discusses and defends poetry and gives us a definition compendious enough to require quite a long statement. It is in verse, and as you will see it requires to be set in verse form:

> If one
> Is forced to stop upon a word because
> The eye or ear is caught there; if a phrase
> Creates a visible image in the mind;
> If by a fractional motion of a form
> The heart is stirred; or if the sense of beauty
> Dilates in pleasure at the artifice;
> And if by repetition, emphasis,
> And open predomination of device
> These forms are made overt and multiplied,
> Then what one reads belongs by aim and method
> To rime.[15]

There Karl Shapiro uses the standard signals ("If . . . if . . . if . . . then") and reinforces that structure with the also standard device of making the final introductory clause the longest of them all. The phrases are, otherwise, much the same in length; variety is the product of the music of the verse. This, like all good verse, begs to be read aloud. Indeed, the whole poem begs to be republished.

Perhaps the most astonishing performance in this form of sentence belongs to the poet Conrad Aiken (and by the way, there is no better way to sharpen one's "style" than by reading all the great poets of the language). Here he goes. Test yourself: read straight through and see if you can grasp the syntax:

> I, the restless one, the circler of circles;
> Herdsman and roper of stars, who could not capture
> The secret of self; I who was tyrant to weaklings,
> Striker of children; destroyer of women; corrupter

Of innocent dreamers, and laugher at beauty; I,
Too easily brought to tears and weakness by music,
Baffled and broken by love, the helpless beholder
Of the war in my heart of desire with desire, the struggle
Of hatred with love, terror with hunger; I
Who laughed without knowing the cause of my laughter,
    who grew
Without wishing to grow, a servant to my own body;
Loved without reason the laughter and flesh of a woman,
Enduring such torments to find her! I who at last
Grow weaker, struggle more feebly, relent in my purpose,
Choose for my triumph an easier end, look backward
At earlier conquests; or, caught in the web, cry out
In a sudden and empty despair, 'Tetelestai!'
Pity me, now! I, who was arrogant, beg you![16]

Here the length of utterance is required not because of a sprawling geography or an endless historical expanse or the summation of argument, but because the autobiography of the speaker is an irreducible part of the statement in which he begs for mercy, a sinner. The skeleton of the sentence is "I beg," but some 170 words intervene between those two fundamental pieces of syntax. By the time we get to "beg," we know who is doing the begging, and why. The sentence is a slam-bang success.

The Saga

The third form that a long sentence may take is what may be called The Saga. Here it is evident that the writer is not concerned with architecture, with what the old boys used to call concinnity, but rather with narration in some form, usually narration unified by actor, episode, or mood. Shakespeare is brim full of these thumbnail sketches and hasty histories, simply because the theater requires that the dramatist produce some background for the characters who strut their fitful hour:

        Our last king,
Whose image even but now appear'd to us,

> Was, as you know, by Fortinbras of Norway,
> Thereto prick'd on by a most emulate pride,
> Dar'd to the combat; in which our valiant Hamlet—
> For so this side of our known world esteem'd him—
> Did slay this Fortinbras; who, by a seal'd compact
> Well ratified by law and heraldry,
> Did forfeit, with his life, all those his lands
> Which he stood seiz'd of, to the conqueror;
> Against the which a moiety competent
> Was gaged by our king, which had returned
> To the inheritance of Fortinbras,
> Had he been vanquisher; as, by the same covenant
> And carriage of the articled design
> His fell to Hamlet.[17]

Schoolmarms would call this a run-on sentence, but The Saga has a reason for its length and shape whereas the run-on does not. The Saga swirls about a constant theme; the run-on drifts from thought to thought without program, design, aim, or method. A run-on is verbal doodling; The Saga is more like theme and variations.

There was a disturbance in a seventeenth-century English household that led to the following entry in a diary that the man of the house kept in his own private code (for reasons that will become apparent):

> My wife did towards bedtime begin in a mighty rage from some new matter that she had got in her head, and did most part of the night in bed rant at me in most high terms of threats of publishing my shame, and when I offered to rise would have rose, too, and caused a candle to be light by her all night in the chimney while she ranted, while the knowing myself to have given grounds for it, did make it my business to appease her all I could possibly, and by good words and fair promises did make her very quiet, and so rested all night, and rose with perfect good peace, being heartily afflicted for this folly of mine that did occasion it, but was forced to be silent about the girle, which I had no mind to part with, but much less that the poor girle should be undone by my folly.[18]

Another feature of The Saga has to do with its being a Performance; it finishes with a flourish of some sort, whereas the run-on simply evanesces as the writer's spirit wanes. Pepys's "girle" pops up at the end of his sentence like a veritable *dea ex machina*.

In our last Saga a Greek girl puts the finishing touches on a thoroughly pleasing performance:

> See enough and write it down, I tell myself, and then some morning when the world seems drained of wonder, some day when I am only going through the motions of doing what I am supposed to do, which is write—on that bankrupt morning I will simply open my notebook and there it will all be, a forgotten account with accumulated interest, paid passage to the world out there; dialogue overheard in hotels and elevators and at the hat-check counter in Pavillon (one middle-aged man shows his hat check to another and says, 'That's my old football number'); impressions of Bettina Aptheker and Benjamin Sonnenberg and Teddy ('Mr. Acapulco') Stauffer; careful *aperçus* about tennis bums and failed fashion models and Greek shipping heiresses, one of whom taught me a significant lesson (a lesson I could have learned from F. Scott Fitzgerald, but perhaps we all must meet the very rich for ourselves) by asking, when I arrived to interview her in her orchid-filled sitting room on the second day of a paralyzing New York blizzard, whether it was snowing outside.[19]

The sentence rises to a strong climax by devoting fully one-third of its length to the final entry, and topping that entry with a well rounded periodic structure. This sort of thing is less easy to bring off than you may think.

Planned Chaos

In the year of Our Lord 1391 a minor political appointee with major literary interests responded to an entreaty from "Litel Lowis my sone" to teach him how to work the astrolabe. The result was a charming 15,000-word instruction manual containing such gems of disorder as the following:

> The 13 day of March fil up-on a Saterday per aventure, and,
> at the arising of the sonne, I fond the secounde degree of
> Aries sitting up-on myn est orisonte, al-be-it that it was but
> lite; than fond I the 2 degree of Libra, nadir of my sonne,
> dessending on my west orisonte, up-on which west orisonte
> every day generally, at the sonne ariste, entreth the houre of
> any planete, after which planete the day bereth his name;
> and endeth in the nexte stryk of the plate under the forseide
> west orisonte; and evere, as the sonne climbeth uppere and
> uppere, so goth his nadir dounere and dounere, teching by
> swich strykes the houres of planetes by ordre as they sitten
> in the hevene.[20]

And so he goes, this Chaucer, the first universal poet in our language, one of the fathers of English verse. How could he commit such a crime as 15,000 words of the above clatter? Obviously he was not intent on writing beautifully: his goal was to instruct a youngster, and so he settled for the nuts and bolts, which the youngster had certainly asked for. Chaucer's delicate ear may have been offended, but he accepted that penalty. The result is neither good nor bad but simply useful, like a monkey wrench, or an astrolabe.

Sir Humphrey Gilbert's last voyage, with a fleet of five ships (with such wondrous names—*Delight, Ralegh, Golden Hind, Swallow, Squirrel!*) departed England on June 11, 1583, and dropped anchor at St. John's, Newfoundland, where, on August 5, Sir Humphrey took possession of the land in the name of the Queen. A description of the land and climate was written by a fellow voyager, one Edward Hare, in the standard loose-limbed syntax of the period:

> Even so all hills having their descents, the valleys also and
> low grounds must be likewise hot or temperate, as the
> clime doth give in Newfoundland: though I am of opinion
> that the sun's reflection is much cooled, and cannot be so
> forcible in Newfoundland, nor generally throughout
> America, as in Europe or Africa: by how much the sun in his
> diurnal course from east to west, passeth over (for the

most part) dry land and sandy countries, before he arriveth at the west of Europe or Africa, whereby his motion increaseth heat, with little or no qualification by moist vapours.[21]

Perhaps the secret weapon of this kind of sentence is that it smacks of free and easy conversation; the length of this sentence derives from the author's need to explain the clime of Newfoundland as a product of the global weather system—a concept that seems about three centuries ahead of itself.

Now we come to Richard Weaver's seventeenth century, where the conversational tone becomes unmistakable. Here's how it sounds in one of the most amazing books in any language, the life work of a man who for some forty-seven years scarcely set foot outside the walls of Oxford, where he haunted the Bodleian Library, as you shall see:

> Greater preferment as I could never get, so am I not in debt for it, I have a competency (*laus Deo*) from my noble and munificent patrons, though I live still a collegiate student, as Democritus in his garden, and lead a monastic life, *ipse mihi theatrum*, sequestered from those tumults and troubles of the world, *et tanquam in specula positus* (as he said), in some high place above you all, like *Stoicus sapiens, omnia saecula, praeterita praesentiaque videns, uno velut intuitu,* I hear and see what is done abroad, how others run, ride, turmoil, and macerate themselves in court and country, far from those wrangling lawsuits, *aulae vanitatem, fori ambitionem, ridere mecum soleo,* I laugh at all; 'only secure lest my suit go amiss, my ships perish,' corn and cattle miscarry, trade decay, 'I have no wife nor children good or bad to provide for.'[22]

There is nothing further to say.

In 1653 the world's most famous work on fishing was first published (it quickly went through several editions, for the author was something of a perfectionist). The author—Izaak Walton, of course—was a skilled writer and in some ways the founder of the modern school of biographical writing, but he loved fishing far too much to confuse it with literature. Consequently his style in his most famous work is disarmingly simple and informal:

> There is also in Kent near to *Canterbury*, a *trout*: (called there a *Fordidge* trout) a trout (that bears the name of the Town, where it is usually caught) that is accounted the rarest of Fish, many of them near the bignesse of a *Salmon*, but known by their different colour, and in their best season cut very white; and none of these have been known to be caught with an Angle, unless it were one that was caught by Sir *George Hastings* (an excellent Angler, and now with God), and he hath told me, he thought that *trout* bit not for hunger but wantonness; and it is the rather to be believed, because he then, and many others before him, have been curious to search into their bellies, what the food was by which they lived; and have found out nothing by which they might satisfy their curiosity.[23]

This is no child at work: the sentence is compound-complex to a faretheewell. Walton's sentences typically run a dozen lines or more, because he will not chop his matter into fragments but insists on giving a compendious report in each sentence. The next sentence following, for example, goes on to sum up all that is known about this trout's eating habits and their relation to the seasons. The informality attained through the use of long, loose structures is a conscious goal of Walton when he writes about something so relaxed and delightful as angling; in his biographies he writes a shorter sentence and achieves a straighter narrative flow, at times sounding very like a modern journalist. The trend had started: seventy years later, around 1723, Daniel Defoe to all intents and purposes invented modern journalism with his *Journal of the Plague Year*.

A hundred years after Defoe another Englishman, also a novelist, invented modern sentimental claptrap and made liberal use of gangling messy sentences to express his welter of emotions. As witness:

But, happy Sissy's happy children loving her; all children loving her; she, grown learned in childish lore; thinking no innocent and pretty fancy ever to be despised; trying hard to know her humbler fellow-creatures, and to beautify their lives of machinery and reality with those imaginative graces and delights, without which the heart of infancy will wither up, the sturdiest physical manhood will be morally stark death, and the plainest national prosperity figures can show will be the Writing on the Wall,—she holding this course as part of no fantastic vow, or bond, or brotherhood, or sister-hood, or pledge, or covenant, or fancy dress, or fancy fair; but simply as a duty to be done,—did Louisa see these things of herself?[24]

"She" is one of "these things"? "Imaginative graces and delights" are the only things sustaining the "national prosperity"? "Sister-hood" or "covenant" can somehow be the antithesis of "duty"? "She" did Louisa see?—But we cannot go on, as Nock once said, lest haply we should pewk.

We have seen Will Percy at work, before, along the banks and levees of the Mississippi. Much earlier, in 1918, during the Great War, he wrote to his father from France, and wrote one of the very few really long sentences that you can find in epistolary literature. The complexity and disorganization of the syntax (strange brothers) are his means of describing the Dickensian con-fusion of the battlefield:

In the mad welter of shell holes and filth and mud emerge, like prehistoric animals from the slime of creation, the wrecks of battles lost and won—shelters of elephant iron, for in the waterlogged land trenches could not be dug; concrete pillboxes torn apart till the iron ribs shattered in gigantic explosions, tanks fantastic and terrible, that had crawled to the roadside or into a shell hole to die (you could not believe they belonged to men till you looked inside and saw the skeletons still by the wheel and the guns); planes that crashed down doubtless into the midst of hurley-burley; shells of all sizes; exploded; duds, used and unused, hel-mets, coats, equipment, belts of ammunition, these were

> down broadcast over the loblolly and in and around and
> across the inextricable confusion, pattern without plan, ran
> the barbed-wire, a crown of thorns on the mangled
> landscape.[25]

He starts with things nicely under control—a formal inversion
puffed out by an interpolation—but gradually loses his grip on
the sentence (or seems to: it is done for effect) and, two-thirds of
the way through ("shells of all sizes"), loses control of the punctuation so that we are surprised to find another syntax governing after
shells: the list is no longer a list of nouns in apposition with
"wrecks," but now becomes a list of nouns that will be the compound subject of a new main clause ("these were down broadcast"). The final main clause is introduced almost surreptitiously
("these were down broadcast over the loblolly and in and around
and across the inextricable confusion, pattern without plan, ran
the barbed-wire"). The final clause is all complicated up with a
second formal inversion ("in and around . . . ran the barbed-
wire") and then an inversion of the appositive structure ("pattern
without plan . . . the barbed-wire"). A highly successful performance, we say, though LeRoy Percy on receiving the letter may
have thought his boy had lost his marbles.

   A slightly tipsy citizen of Dublin is reminiscing in a pub one
evening:

> For instance, when the evicted tenants' question, then at its
> first inception, bulked largely in people's minds though, it
> goes without saying, not contributing a copper or pinning
> his faith absolutely to its dictums, some of which wouldn't
> exactly hold water, he at the outset in principle, at all events,
> was in thorough sympathy with peasant possession, as voicing
> the trend of modern opinion, a partiality, however, which,
> realising his mistake, he was subsequently partially cured of,
> and even was twitted with going a step further than Michael
> Davitt in the striking views he at one time inculcated as a
> backtothelander, which was one reason he strongly resented
> the innuendo put upon him in so barefaced a fashion at the
> gathering of the clans in Barney Kiernan's so that he, though

often considerably misunderstood and the least pugnacious
of mortals, be it repeated, departed from his customary habit
to give him (metaphorically) one in the gizzard though so far
as politics themselves were concerned, he was only too conscious of the casualties invariably resulting from propaganda
and displays of mutual animosity and the misery and suffering it entailed as a foregone conclusion on fine young fel-
lows, chiefly, destruction of the fittest, in a word.[26]

That's a pretty effective way to mimic the endless banal saloon
chatter of Joyce's time and country. The cute little irony at the
end—"in a word"—is a bit of self-criticism, yes?

Our last bird of chaos is a truly virtuoso performance concerning a sudden death:

She was a lady of high degree who had fallen not out of
fashion, exactly, but out of respectable repute because on her
wedding night, in Biarritz or Nice, her ideally handsome,
youthful and well-born bridegroom, known as Boy Fenwick,
I believe, leapt out of the bridal suite to his death on the
stones of the courtyard below, which caused a considerable
sensation, probably making headlines in two nations, mainly
because of the heroine (Iris March) announcing to the press
that 'Boy died for purity' and declining to go into further
details on this intriguing matter.[27]

Now isn't that fun? Williams seeks to let the air out of these
people's tires and does so by making use of a very limp sentence
in which just about everything is slightly out of focus or
misplaced, as if he really didn't care all that much. "She was a
lady . . ." is no way to start a sentence that is to tell us that Boy
jumped out of a window to his death, unless, you see, you don't
happen to think that Boy was very important. You don't think
much of the lady, either, because she has fallen "not out of
fashion"—a nice inversion, that—but out of genteel odor, and
you're not sure whether the wedding night was in Biarritz or
Nice, and you're not sure whether her bridegroom was named
Boy Fenwick though you "believe" he was, and the whole

episode is tucked into a relative pronoun ("which") that you know very well shouldn't be made to serve such onerous duty, but the event was just an "item" and so deserves nothing more than a "which" clause, and the result of the suicide was not a scandal but a "considerable sensation," such as one kicks up when one sets fire to the potted palms in the lobby, and it made headlines "probably"—who cares?—in two nations, which don't matter enough to be named, because the lady said something enigmatic and then clammed up, terminating discussion of this—death? suicide? tragedy? Greek drama? amazing turn of events?—no, "this intriguing matter," much on a par, let us say, with cheating at whist. Well done!

The Four-Masted Schooner

This last type of long sentence exhibits one feature in high profile: a splendid fulsomeness. Not only must a sentence be syntactically strong to qualify for membership in this company, but also it must be swollen in all its members, like a sufferer of the dropsy. As Weaver noted, we find our best samples of this monster in earlier times, though one nineteenth-century genius, Walter Bagehot, was a great practitioner of this kind of spaciousness. Here's Sir Walter Ralegh, in 1591, getting under way with his report on a naval engagement:

> Because the rumors are diversely spread, as well in England as in the Low Countries and elsewhere, of this late encounter between Her Majesty's ships and the Armada of Spain; and that the Spaniards according to their usual manner fill the world with their vainglorious vaunts, making great appearance of victories, when on the contrary themselves are most commonly and shamefully beaten and dishonored; thereby hoping to possess the ignorant multitude by anticipating and forerunning false reports; it is agreeable with all good reason, for manifestation of the truth, to overcome falsehood and untruth, that the beginning, continuance, and success of this late honorable encounter of Sir Richard Gren-

ville and other Her Majesty's captains, with the Armada of Spain, should be truly set down and published without partiality or false imaginations.[28]

Much of the fulsomeness in this sentence derives from elaboration of the various elements, a foretaste of the "balanced style" of the eighteenth century. Ralegh deals much in pairs: in England and in the Low Countries, commonly and shamefully, beaten and dishonored, anticipating and forerunning, beginning and continuance and success (a pair and a half), set down and published, partiality or imaginations. In strong hands this style attains a certain mightiness.

However, Ralegh, great sea captain though he was, could never match another of his countrymen in handling The Four-Masted Schooner. Listen to the champ:

> First, when a city shall be as it were besieged and blocked about, her navigable river infested, inroads and incursions round, defiance and battle oft rumoured to be marching up even to her walls, and suburb trenches, that then the people, or the greater part, more than at other times, wholly taken up with the study of highest and most important matters to be reformed, should be disputing, reasoning, reading, inventing, discoursing, even to a rarity, and admiration, things not before discoursed or written of, argues first a singular good will, contentedness, and confidence in your prudent foresight, and safe government, Lords and Commons; and from thence derives itself to a gallant bravery and well-grounded contempt of their enemies, as if there were no small number of as great spirits among us, as his was, who when Rome was nigh besieged by Hannibal, being in the city, bought that piece of ground at no cheap rate whereon Hannibal himself encamped his own regiment.[29]

Once again, rock-solid syntax and riotous fulsomeness combine to produce a masterly effect. The bulk and stateliness of the sentence accord perfectly with the solemnity and power of the argument. You don't dispatch a four-masted schooner to trawl for mackerel.

A hundred years later a working journalist (and poet, critic, biographer, moralist) exemplified this style, though with the streamlining that would lead eventually to the stripped-down manner of the twentieth century:

> The imagination of the first authors of lyrick poetry was vehement and rapid, and their knowledge various and extensive. Living in an age when science had been little cultivated, and when the minds of their auditors, not being accustomed to accurate inspection, were easily dazzled by glaring ideas, they applied themselves to instruct, rather by short sentences and striking thoughts, than by regular argumentation; and finding attention more successfully excited by sudden sallies and unexpected exclamations, than by the more artful and placid beauties of methodical deduction, they loosed their genius to its own course, passed from one sentiment to another without expressing the intermediate ideas, and roved at large over the ideal world with such lightness and agility that their footsteps are scarcely to be traced.[30]

That's good Dr. Johnson on an average day. He tossed that stuff off by the furlong. Note that his sentence is compound and the two halves are matched in syntax ("Living in an age . . . they applied themselves . . . ; and finding attention . . . they loosed their genius . . ."). That firm and elegant structure goes a long way towards giving this sentence its dignity.

A hundred years later the gifted and indefatigable Walter Bagehot, editor of *The Economist* (London), undertook a whopping big sentence in describing the miseries of the emancipated Negroes after our War Between the States:

> Liberated from their old masters and unable to find new ones for themselves,—helpless with the helplessness natural to men who have never been taught or allowed to initiate or arrange their own actions, and not knowing how to set about any work, which is not prepared for them and ordered to them,—calling, therefore, for support and aid upon those who conferred this impoverishing freedom upon them, but

calling for the most part in vain, because their liberators, with the best will in the world, simply *cannot* provide sustenance or organise employment for such vast and sudden numbers,—little inclined to labour at all, as might be expected, because labour in their minds is associated with slavery and liberty with idleness,—despised and not loved (to say the least) by the great mass of the Northerners, and actually detested by the Irish,—hated at once with the mortification of defeat and the bitterness of destitution, by those to whom they were a short time ago both slaves and wealth,—and exposed, therefore, on all sides to ill-treatment and neglect against which, and the consequences of which, nothing short of ubiquitous omnipotence could effectually protect four millions of suddenly emancipated serfs,—these unhappy victims of philanthropy and civil war are dying, we are told, by thousands; numbers are shot on the slightest provocation or from sheer brutality by the miscellaneous ruffians who abound there; numbers more sink under disease and famine; numbers emigrate northward, to fare no better; the law does not protect them; the civil authorities will not; the military authorities cannot.[31]

Bagehot paints on a panoramic scale but never loses track of the structure of his sentence, which he keeps limpidly clear to the reader, so clear in fact that no adult reader should have any trouble recognizing the syntactical elements as he runs through the sentence for the first time. Phrase by phrase Bagehot uses very straightforward diction and style, giving swiftness to his writing; and by doubling up and using pairs of words with great frequency he achieves that fulsome flair that is one of the traits of The Four-Masted Schooner. He wrote thousands of pages on hundreds of different topics, each page evincing the same headlong energy and universal grasp of detail, and making use constantly of such large structures as above. It was in his nature.

Finally, here's a glorious example of the full style and the all-encompassing vision. Once again it is the American landscape that inspires the spacious rhetoric, and we pick up the story as the settlers of this continent first found their way to the million square miles of fertile earth beyond the eastern mountains. This was published in 1903, the work of an American historian, a Southern conservative, a college president (Princeton):

> Northwestward along the valleys of the Mohawk and the Delaware into the land of the Iroquois which Sullivan had harried,—where Sir William Johnson had reigned in days gone by over red men and white; straight towards the heart of the West along the upper courses of the Potomac, through the difficult country through which Braddock had gone his blundering way, to Fort Pitt and the lands by the Ohio; through the long forests to the fair Kentucky; down the valleys opened by the spreading tributaries of the Tennessee, and through the forests beyond to the Cumberland, whither the men who had ridden the passes to King's Mountain had shown the way; around the southern end of the great Appalachians to the plains by the Gulf,—wherever the mountains opened or a way could be made, ever-increasing bands of emigrants essayed the long journey every open season, seeking new homes at the heart of the lands where once the French had had their posts and garrisons,—until there began to be communities beyond the mountains big enough to count in affairs: communities in whose behalf peace and government must be provided, and a way of intercourse and sympathy between East and West to which the great mountain ranges should be no effectual barrier.[32]

Yes, that was Woodrow Wilson before he fell from grace and went into politics. A thoroughly trained rhetorician from his youth, Wilson commanded a lordly and spirited style with energy aplenty. Here, for instance, he could have stopped after "posts and garrisons" and had himself a nice day's work, but he went the extra mile, starting with that sudden "until . . ." and giving us the far distant completion of this enormous movement of people: the establishment of community, peace, and government in the formerly savage and unknown—vast and howling—wilderness.

CHAPTER FOUR

Kick Up Your Heels

T HE Four-Masted Schooner needs oceans of prose to sail in, but other devices, such as the various humorous devices we'll turn to now, are appropriate to all forms of writing, from a personal letter to a book on moral theology. There are occasions, to be sure, when humor is not appropriate; and some audiences discourage it. IBM once fired someone for preparing a ribald mock advertisement for one of the company's products. But at *National Review* humor is nearly always in order, even in the publisher's memo announcing that Labor Day, although of syndicalist origin, would be a full holiday, or the housekeeping notice that began, "Unless it is proved that a band of highly literate vagabonds descended upon and took nest in our conference room . . ." Long before *The New York Times* replaced Who, What, When, and Where with soft news, James F. Clarity could write that many but not all of the delegates to the United Nations had abandoned their native costumes: "Gone . . . were the colorful raiments of the Bhutanese and the flowing robes of the African delegates. There was hardly a fez in view. A notable exception was William F. Buckley, Jr. . . . who wore a dark suit, rep tie, and button-down shirt."[1]

Observation is again the starting point, but observation with a twist. If two details or the sounds of two words brush against each other in a way you had not foreseen, instead of suppressing one of them, make the most of the reverberations. If a list of three items would make the serious point, you can add four (or twenty) more to give your reader a treat—while still making the serious point.

Some devices, particularly puns, have no uses outside the humorous; they would not be appropriate in, say, a condolence letter or an editorial about casualties of war. But many of the devices we have mentioned elsewhere in this book are suitable to a variety of contexts; they are rhetorical containers that can be filled up with different sorts of matter, tragic or comic, uplifting or ironic. The great period beginning "This royal throne of kings," which we quoted in Chapter Three, is a serious and moving enumeration of partial synonyms. Here is a different sort of catalogue:

> 'I wish to complain about this parrot, what I purchased not half an hour ago from this very boutique.'
> 'Oh yes, the Norwegian blue. What's wrong with it?'
> 'I'll tell you what's wrong with it: it's dead, that's what's wrong with it.' . . .
> 'It's probably pining for the fjords.' . . .
> 'It's not pining, it's passed on. This parrot is no more. It has ceased to be. It's expired and gone to meet its Maker.
> 'This is a late parrot. It's a stiff. Bereft of life, it rests in peace. If you hadn't nailed it to its perch it would be pushing up the daisies. It's rung down the curtain and joined the choir invisible.
> 'This is an ex-parrot.'[2]

At that, the Pythons left out a few possibilities: kicked the bucket, cashed in its chips, turned up its toes . . .

Cyrano de Bergerac never leaves anything out; once he has got started, he carries on to the very end. A foolish viscount has sought to insult him by telling him his nose is very large. "Is that all?" asks Cyrano:

> One could have said—O Lord—so many things,
> While varying the tone. For instance, sir:
> Aggressive: 'Had I such a nose as yours,
> I'd have it amputated right away.'

Solicitous: 'It must dip in your cup.
You ought to get yourself a special mug.'
Descriptive: 'It's a rock! A peak! A cape!
I said a cape? It's a *peninsula!*'
Inquisitive: 'That box—what is it for?
A writing desk? Perhaps a scissors case?'
Benevolent: 'Are you so fond of birds
That you have had a care to offer them
A kindly perch to rest their little feet?'
Combative: 'Tell me, when you light your pipe,
And when the smoke comes streaming from your nose
Does not your neighbor cry out, Chimney fire!?'
Advisory: 'Take care the weight does not
Unbalance you so that you fall head first.'
Benign: 'You ought to find a parasol
To guard it from the bright rays of the sun.'
Pedantic: 'Aristophanes's beast,
Yclept the Hippocampelephantocamelos,
Should be the only animal whose face
Hefts up such mounds of flesh upon such bone.'
Impertinent: 'That hook—is it in style?
At least it must be handy as a hat rack.'
Emphatic: 'But for the *mistral*, no wind
Could give that whole enormous nose a cold.'
Dramatic: 'When it bleeds, the Red Sea flows.'
Admiring: 'What a sign for perfume shops!'
Poetic: 'That's a shell? And are you Triton?'
Naïf: 'When may we view the monument?'
Respectful: 'Sir, allow me to salute you;
That's what you might call frontage on the street.'
Bucolic: 'Say, is that a nose? No way.
A giant turnip, or a dwarf muskmelon.'
Commanding: 'Train your cannon on their horse!'
Direct: 'Why don't you enter it when next
We have a lottery? You'd win first prize.'
Or finally, like Pyramus, all sobs:
'This nose has quite destroyed the harmony
Of its good master's face. The traitor blushes.'
There's the sort of thing you might have said,
Had you but had some learning or some wit.[3]

If we had a hat with a plume—a *panache*—like Cyrano's, we would take it off for a moment of silence.

In our own day, Tom Wolfe is famous for his lists—"a crocus sack full of revolvers, ice picks, fish knives, switchblades, hatchets, blackjacks, gravity knives, straight razors, hand grenades, blow guns, bazookas, Molotov cocktails, tank rippers,"[4] those being some of the things the Mau-Mauer tells the Flak Catcher "I took off my boys last night"—but even Wolfe normally mixes them up with other devices:

> *Mmmmmmmmmmmmmmmmm.* These are nice. Little Roquefort cheese morsels rolled in crushed nuts. Very tasty. Very subtle. It's the way the dry sackiness of the nuts tiptoes up against the dour savor of the cheese that is so nice, so subtle. Wonder what the Black Panthers eat here on the hors d'oeuvre trail? Do the Panthers like little Roquefort cheese morsels rolled in crushed nuts this way, and asparagus tips in mayonnaise dabs, and *meatballs petites au Coq Hardi*, all of which are at this very moment being offered to them on gadrooned silver platters by maids in black uniforms with hand-ironed white aprons . . .[5]

Internal repetitions ("nice . . . Very subtle . . . so nice, so subtle") and parodies both of the out-of-control food writer ("dry sackiness . . . dour savor") and of the naïvely sophisticated party-goer wondering how other people live lead up to the list of heavily modified nouns, at which point the casual syntax is brought to an end by a formal relative clause.

Mencken too likes to pile up examples—both the particulars of his indictment and exaggerated comparisons:

> It is as if the Civil War stamped out every last bearer of the torch, and left only a mob of peasants on the field. One thinks of Asia Minor, resigned to Armenians, Greeks and wild swine, of Poland abandoned to the Poles. In all that gargantuan paradise of the fourth-rate there is not a single picture gallery worth going into, or a single orchestra capable of playing the nine symphonies of Beethoven, or a single

opera-house, or a single theater devoted to decent plays, or a single public monument that is worth looking at, or a single workshop devoted to the making of beautiful things. Once you have counted James Branch Cabell (a lingering survivor of the *ancien régime*: a scarlet dragon-fly imbedded in opaque amber) you will not find a single Southern prose writer who can actually write. And once you have—but when you come to critics, musical composers, painters, sculptors, architects and the like, you will have to give it up, for there is not even a bad one between the Potomac mud-flats and the Gulf. Nor a historian. Nor a philosopher. Nor a theologian. Nor a scientist. In all these fields the South is an awe-inspiring blank—a brother to Portugal, Serbia and Albania.[6]

Before he has finished the essay, Mencken has run through a veritable almanac of depressing places: "an intellectual Gobi or Lapland . . . One could no more imagine a Lee or a Washington in the Virginia of today than one could imagine a Huxley in Nicaragua . . . as if the scene were the Balkans or the China Coast." (And before our Southern readers start throwing rotten okra and dead catfish, let us note the date this was written—1917—and quote Mencken's own later preface: "[This essay] produced a ferocious reaction in the South, and I was belabored for months, and even years afterward in a very extravagant manner. . . . On the heels of the violent denunciations of the elder Southerners there soon came a favorable response from the more civilized youngsters, and there is reason to believe that my attack had something to do with that revival of Southern letters which followed in the middle 1920s.")

The catalogue combines with epic exaggeration to produce this jeremiad against the role Michelangelo plays in a guided tour of Italy:

> In this connection I wish to say one word about Michael Angelo Buonarotti. I used to worship the mighty genius of Michael Angelo—that man who was great in poetry, painting, sculpture, architecture—great in everything he undertook. But I do not want Michael Angelo for breakfast—for

luncheon—for dinner—for tea—for supper—for between
meals. I like a change, occasionally. In Genoa, he designed
everything; in Milan he or his pupils designed everything;
he designed the Lake of Como; in Padua, Verona, Venice,
Bologna, who did we ever hear of, from guides, but
Michael Angelo? In Florence, he painted everything,
designed everything, nearly, and what he did not design
he used to sit on a favorite stone and look at, and they
showed us the stone. In Pisa he designed everything but
the old shot-tower, and they would have attributed that to
him if it had not been so awfully out of the perpendicular.
He designed the piers of Leghorn and the custom-house
regulations of Civita Vecchia. But, here [in Rome]—here it
is frightful. He designed St. Peter's; he designed the Pope;
he designed the Pantheon, the uniform of the Pope's sol-
diers, the Tiber, the Vatican, the Coliseum, the Capitol, the
Tarpeian Rock, the Barberini Palace, St. John Lateran, the
Campagna, the Appian Way, the Seven Hills, the Baths of
Caracalla, the Claudian Aqueduct, the Cloaca Maxima—
the eternal bore designed the Eternal City, and unless all
men and books do lie, he painted everything in it! Dan
said the other day to the guide, 'Enough, enough, enough!
Say no more! Lump the whole thing! say that the Creator
made Italy from designs by Michael Angelo.'[7]

The items catalogued can be other rhetorical devices, such
as maxims and allusions. When it comes to maxims, Sancho
Panza is the all-time champ:

> In the next place, *Sancho,* said the Knight, do not over-
> lard your common Discourse with that glut of Proverbs,
> which you mix in it continually; for though Proverbs are
> properly concise and pithy Sentences, yet as thou bringst 'em
> in, in such a huddle, by the Head and Shoulders, thou
> makest 'em look like so many Absurdities.
>
> Alas! Sir, quoth *Sancho,* this is a disease that Heaven
> alone can cure; for I've more Proverbs than will fill a Book;
> and when I talk, they crowd so thick and fast to my Mouth,
> that they quarrel which shall get out first; so that my Tongue
> is forc'd to let 'em out as fast, first come first serv'd, though

nothing to my Purpose. But henceforwards I'll set a Watch on my Mouth, and let none fly out, but such as shall befit the Gravity of my Place. For in a rich Man's House the Cloth is soon laid; where there's Plenty the Guests can't be empty. A Blot's no Blot till 'tis hit. He's safe who stands under the Bells; you can't eat your Cake and have your Cake; and Store's no Sore.

Go on, go on, Friend, said Don *Quixote*, thread, tack, stitch on, heap Proverb on Proverb, out with 'em, Man, spew them out! There's no body coming. My Mother whips me, and I whip the Gigg. I warn thee to forbear foisting in a Rope of Proverbs every where, and thou blunder'st out a whole Litany of old saws, as much to the Purpose as *the last Year's Snow.* . . . Oh! as for that, quoth *Sancho*, I can do well enough . . . for there's a remedy for all things but Death. And since I've the Power, I'll do what I list; for as the Saying is, *He whose Father is judge, goes safe* to his Trial. And as I am a Governor, I hope I am somewhat higher than a Judge. New Lords, new Laws. Ay, ay, ay, let them come as they will, and play at Bopeep. Let 'em backbite me to my Face, I'll bite-back the biters. Let 'em come for wool, and I'll send 'em home shorn. Whom God loves, his House happy proves. The rich Man's Follies pass for wise Sayings in this World. So I, being rich, d'you see, and a Governor, and free-hearted too into the Bargain, as I intend to be, I shall have no faults at all. 'Tis so, daub yourself with Honey, and you'll never want flies. What a Man has, so much he's sure of, said my old Grannam; and who shall hang the bell about the Cat's Neck?

Confound thee, cry'd Don *Quixote*, for an eternal Proverb-voiding Swag-belly. Threescore thousand Belzebubs take thee, and thy damn'd nauseous Rubbish. Thou hast been this Hour stringing them together, like so many Ropes of Onions, and poisoning and racking me with 'em. I dare say, these wicked Proverbs will one Day bring thee to the Gallows. . . .[8]

The fractured maxim has a special place in comic writing, and few people fracture a maxim like Bertie Wooster. Bertie fortunately has Jeeves to come along and put the pieces back together:

'Yes, I recall the Sipperley case. He couldn't bring himself to the scratch. A marked coldness of the feet, was there not? I recollect you saying he was letting—what was it?—letting something do something. Cats entered into it, if I am not mistaken.'

'Letting "I dare not" wait upon "I would," sir.'

'That's right. But how about the cats?'

'Like the poor cat i' the adage, sir.'

'Exactly. It beats me how you think up these things.'[9]

Myles na Gopaleen has a different way with a stock phrase, concocting a lengthy story to lead up to a twist on the phrase, as in the one about two men who buy a bull and a farm, only to have the venture prove madly uneconomical. The conclusion? "'You had better eradicate the whole wretched project,' Keats said acidly, 'brute and ranch.'"[10]

Note that both elements here, the words actually written and the ones they are meant to suggest, work in context. This is the criterion for distinguishing between the true pun and the sort of formulation typically accompanied by an insincere "No pun intended." Even good puns (ones displaying a certain level of intellectual cultivation) are not to everyone's taste—one man's Mede is another man's Persian. Reading the sports headlines in the daily newspaper can induce a powerful allergy. But good puns do exist—like another offering from Myles na Gopaleen, about a duel which is ended by the second's throwing a small portable stove at the combatants' blades at a critical moment. "You saved my life!" says the duelist. "You're tops!"

The second replies: "Primus inter parries."[11]

Metaphor and simile will also serve a comic turn. In fact, the writer must take care that they do not do so in spite of him: the metaphor he has not visualized before committing it to print can spring to life in a grotesque way, like the war babies in Chapter Two. Furthermore, there are fashions in metaphor as in sentence length and diction, and metaphors that would have been applauded in the eighteenth century would be laughed at today, even if they were correctly worked out to the last detail. Fowler gives this example from Samuel Richardson:

> Tost to and fro by the high winds of passionate control, I behold the desired port, the single state, into which I would fain steer; but am kept off by the foaming billows of a brother's & sister's envy, & by the raging winds of a supposed invaded authority; while I see in Lovelace, the rocks on one hand, & in Solmes, the sands on the other; & tremble, lest I should split upon the former or strike upon the latter.[12]

Not a word misplaced, but the modern reader says, Cut! (The modern reader's grandfather would have said, Cut the cackle and get to the horses.) But the writer will not be hampered by this change in tastes if his context is not solemn:

> Or, to expand the statement a little, there was a fight, if not a war at least a long, sustained battle; heavy artillery was brought into play on both sides; men fought in that battle with the kind of bitterness and acrimony that human beings appear to reserve for those occasions on which brother fights brother, cousin fights cousin, Damon—yes, it was often so, as I can testify from personal experience—fights Pythias. For a long while smoke hung thick over the field of battle, so that visibility was poor and there was great confusion on the part of the observing public, not merely as to how, at any given moment, the battle was going, but even as to what precisely the fighting was about—as to what exactly was getting decided, as to what actually the victor, once he emerged triumphant, would have won. Moreover, so thick was the smoke that the combatants themselves often became hazy in their minds, even differed among themselves, as to who was whose enemy and as to the sense in which this or that 'enemy,' if he was an enemy, was an enemy.[13]

Kendall laces his extended metaphor about the battle over Joe McCarthy with plenty of other devices—quotation, allusion, repetition—as does the Connecticut Yankee, describing a young woman's tendency to say everything she has to say at one go:

> I was gradually coming to have a mysterious and shuddery reverence for this girl; for now-a-days whenever she pulled out from the station and got her train fairly started on one of those horizonless transcontinental sentences of hers, it was borne in upon me that I was standing in the awful presence of the Mother of the German Language. I was so impressed with this, that sometimes when she began to empty one of these sentences on me I unconsciously took the very attitude of reverence, and stood uncovered; and if words had been water, I had been drowned, sure. She had exactly the German way: whatever was in her mind to be delivered, whether a mere remark, or a sermon, or a cyclopedia, or the history of a war, she would get it into a single sentence or die. Whenever the literary German dives into a sentence, that is the last you are going to see of him till he emerges on the other side of his Atlantic with his verb in his mouth.[14]

Whereas Willmoore Kendall used one extended metaphor, Mark Twain uses three substantial ones. However, there is nothing mixed about them; each is neatly folded and stowed away before the next one is pulled out.

Once upon a time personification was usable in the most elevated contexts—think of the Greeks' rosy-fingered dawn, or the characters in any allegory. This has grown uncommon in our

> undisciplined
> And concert-going age,
> So lacking in conviction
> It cannot take pure fiction,
> And what it wants from you
> Are rumors partly true;[15]

but we can still use it for comic effect, e.g., "Hambledon made a metaphorical grab at his escaping temper, smacked its head, and pushed it behind him."[16] Manning Coles did not need that "metaphorical," but the image survives the doubly dotted *i* and crossed *t*.

Here is a sample in which an abstraction is personified while the young man chosen as the illustration is in the process subtly depersonalized. Hooper is Captain Ryder's slovenly and undereducated subaltern:

> In the weeks that we were together Hooper became a symbol to me of Young England, so that whenever I read some public utterance proclaiming what Youth demanded in the Future and what the world owed to Youth, I would test these general statements by substituting 'Hooper' and seeing if they still seemed as plausible. Thus in the dark hour before reveille I sometimes pondered: 'Hooper Rallies,' 'Hooper Hostels,' 'International Hooper Cooperation' and 'the Religion of Hooper.' He was the acid test of all these alloys.[17]

W. H. Auden lures various Egos and the Super-Ego out of the dark Freudian unconscious and takes them for a ride:

> If a large lady carelessly, but not intentionally, treads on my corn during a subway rush hour, what goes on in my mind can be expressed dramatically as follows:
>
> SELF: (*in whom the physical sensation of pain has become the mental passion of anger*): 'Care for my anger! Do something about it!'
>
> COGNITIVE EGO: 'You are angry because of the pain caused by this large lady who, carelessly but not intentionally, has trodden on your corn. If you decide to relieve your feelings, you can give her a sharp kick on the ankle without being noticed.'
>
> SELF: 'Kick her.'
>
> SUPER-EGO: . . . 'Unintentional wrongs must not be avenged. Ladies must not be kicked. Control your anger!'
>
> LADY: (*noticing what she has done*): 'I beg your pardon! I hope I didn't hurt you.'
>
> SELF: 'Kick her!'
>
> SUPER-EGO: 'Smile! Say "Not at all, Madam."'
>
> VOLITIONAL EGO: (*to the appropriate voluntary muscles*): *either* 'Kick her!'
> *or* 'Smile! Say "Not at all, Madam."'[18]

In previous chapters we have seen some serious uses of the juxtaposition of unlike items, but it can also be pure fun:

> [The inhabitants of] the picturesque little settlement of Wood
> Hills . . . live in commodious houses, standing in their own
> grounds, and enjoy so many luxuries—such as gravel soil,
> main drainage, electric light, telephone, baths (h. and c.), and
> company's own water, that you might be pardoned for imagin-
> ing life to be so ideal for them that no possible improvement
> could be added to their lot. Mrs Willoughby Smethurst was
> under no such delusion. What Wood Hills needed to make it
> perfect, she realized, was Culture. Material comforts are all
> very well, but, if the *summum bonum* is to be achieved, the
> Soul also demands a look in, and it was Mrs Smethurst's
> unfaltering resolve that never while she had her strength
> should the Soul be handed the loser's end. It was her inten-
> tion to make Wood Hills a centre of all that was most cul-
> tivated and refined, and, golly! how she had succeeded.[19]

But Wodehouse's prize verbal juxtapositions spring from the juxtaposition of his most famous characters, Bertie and Jeeves:

> 'I am inclined to think that there must be some mis-
> take, and that this bird who has been calling here is some
> different variety of Fink-Nottle. The chap I know wears
> horn-rimmed spectacles and has a face like a fish. How does
> that check up with your data?'
> 'The gentleman who came to the flat wore horn-rimmed
> spectacles, sir.'
> 'And looked like something on a slab?'
> 'Possibly there was a certain suggestion of the piscine,
> sir.'[20]

All these devices find a triumphant home in a passage that
attempts the hardest of forms to bring off: the parody of a piece of
writing that is already on the outer limits of stream-of-conscious-
ness. Here, James Joyce meets modern computer language:

> In endless loops my grandfather/father/son lies, their bones
> of CORAL made. Arrays! Arrays brave Fortranbras and tak
> the low code while Putney Bridge is falling down. I see hell!
> ICL! I see hell in your eyes; one single-tender glance. All
> hands off DEC as we cross the Hudson, the river of low
> returns. Seekest thou the sweet Honeywell, well, well or the

feedholes of a naked Burroughs lunch? Holy Macro, Mother of GOD, things Rank Xerox and Herb Grosch in nature possess us merely. That it should come to this. Not three months merged. Nay, not so much. The one true road beckons. Una vecchio. Univaccio. O Lord, sperry us from their fastrandy forcesales. I hear the crash of distant drums. Mauchly eckertistical! Is the END so near? Halt-tape-jam-break-fast. 4K the lot.[21]

Repetition, allusion, pun, macaronic language . . . We should add that this sample is for demonstration purposes only; do not attempt this dish in your home kitchen unless you have a great deal of experience, and a good insurance policy.

After an overwhelming performance like that it is a relief to remember that much humor aims to elicit the smile of recognition rather than the gasp of admiration. Here is a closing passage that depends mostly on observation of incongruities, with only a couple of bells and whistles added:

> When a child falls over a chair, its instant reaction will very likely be to say, 'Naughty chair,' and belabour it soundly with whatever first comes to hand. That is apt to strike the grown-up Adam, who knows more than the child about the nature of inanimate matter, as funny: but if Adam is sensible he will take the stick away and not encourage the child to expect the material universe to accommodate itself to his wishes.
>
> The grown-up Adam, having laughed at the child, may then go to Piccadilly Tube Station with the intention of taking a train to Stanmore. With his mind fixed on the Test Match or the sins of the Government, he may neglect to consult the indicator which is saying plainly that the train now at the platform is going to Watford, and when, having passed Baker Street in a fond illusion, he looks up at the next station and finds that it is not St. John's Wood but Marylebone, he will mutter savagely that he has got into 'the wrong train.' Neither will it for a moment occur to him that what he is saying is as absurd as what the child said. But what is wrong with the train? In the eyes of God and London Passenger

Transport, it is a perfectly good train, proceeding on its lawful occasions to the destination appointed for it by a superior power. To be sure, it has got a wrong passenger, who has nobody to blame but himself. But the determination to see the good as evil and the right train as a wrong 'un has entrenched itself in the very core of Adam's language: and it is well for his soul if he confines himself to that merely conventional method of transferring his own errors to the universe, and does not angrily add that 'all these damned trains seem to go to Watford.'[22]

CHAPTER FIVE

The Tools of the Trade

FIGURES—as in figures of speech—are the tools of your trade; and the more you possess and can deploy, the better you will write. A figure is any contrived departure from simple barebones talk, any "erosion" as Ortega said. The phrase "tools of the trade" is a figure in this context, because it clearly does not mean any such thing as the physical instruments a writer uses—pencil, wastebasket, pen, ink, wastebasket, paper, typing keys, dictionary, wastebasket, scissors, glue, cusswords, wastebasket. It suggests, and is intended to suggest, a relation: tools are to the tradesman as figures of speech are to the wordsmith. It is a metaphor, a kind of Trope.

Figures come in two kinds, those that deal with individual words and those that have to do with the arrangement of a number of words. When you plot out and execute an effective arrangement of words, you are scheming: your figure is a Scheme. Your fiddling with individual words produces Tropes. The mastery of figures was one of the five parts of the classical system of rhetoric, and we propose to trot out a few dozen of the most common of them for your inspection.

The object of digging into Schemes and Tropes is not to satisfy some twisted pedantic lust, though the good Lord knows the study of rhetoric has bred pedants thicker than Japanese beetles in the raspberry patch, but instead to make sure you are aware of the resources of language and have confidence in them. That a certain Trope or Scheme has been known since the days of Aristotle and was indeed first named by Aristotle should give you confidence that when you use it you are not exactly sticking your neck out on your own authority. Take the sentence a few lines above: "Tools are to the tradesman as figures of speech are to the wordsmith." That can be improved by omitting the second "are," so that it reads, "Tools are to the tradesman as figures of speech to the wordsmith." That is a Scheme, called ellipsis; it has been known for about 2,500 years. Trust it, use it!

Okay, here we go.

Schemes

Alliteration: heavy use of a given letter or sound at the beginnings of closely connected words.

> These are the times that try men's souls. The summer soldier and the sunshine patriot will, in this crisis, shrink from the service of their country.[1]

Fine for advertisements, pamphlets, political slogans ("Rum, Romanism, and Rebellion"), and comic effect (see almost any column by William Safire), this figure must be used with restraint. Overdone, it becomes ludicrous if not downright annoying.

Anacoluthon: an abrupt shift in syntactical structure so that a sentence does not run to the end as a syntactical whole. See the "Sissy" sentence by Dickens in Chapter Three. Normally a device to express extreme emotion, anacoluthon can also, as in Dickens, betray nothing more serious than dilapidation of the brain.

Anadiplosis: starting a clause with the last word of the preceding clause.

> The tyrant falls before the oligarch, the oligarch is swept aside by democracy, democracy brings liberty, liberty brings license, license brings anarchy, and anarchy invites the tyrant.

Anaphora: starting a sequence of clauses with the same word or the same phrase. This almost barbarically rudimentary device is the stock in trade of evangelists, rabble rousers, and politicians, perhaps because the repetition of a formula at the start of each clause gives them time to think before they proclaim their next nonsequitur. M. L. King's "I have a dream" speech is a cut above the junk-talk because of the undeniable eloquence of the clauses following the stock phrase. A rare and most beauteous instance of anaphora in the hands of our greatest master occurs in *The Merchant of Venice*:

> *Lorenzo.* The moon shines bright. In such a night as this,
> When the sweet wind did gently kiss the trees
> And they did make no noise, in such a night
> Troilus methinks mounted the Troyan walls,
> And sighed his soul toward the Grecian tents,
> Where Cressid lay that night.
> *Jessica.*   In such a night
> Did Thisbe fearfully o'ertrip the dew,
> And saw the lion's shadow ere himself,
> And ran dismay'd away.
> *Lorenzo.*   In such a night
> Stood Dido with a willow in her hand
> Upon the wild sea banks, and waft her love
> To come again to Carthage.
> *Jessica.*   In such a night
> Medea gathered the enchanted herbs
> That did renew old Aeson. . . .[2]

and so through three more speeches. Anaphora sets up a powerful rhythmic structure, something akin to an incantation—which is why we think of it as such a basic device as to be almost primitive. But the OOM-pa-pa-pa OOM-pa-pa-pa of the medicine men and the rainmakers is nonetheless effective and deeply moving; anaphora should be used but only when it's your business to stir emotions.

Anastrophe: inversion of the normal word order. If you need to highlight a word, you should contrive to place it at the head or the tail of the sentence. If this requires writing somewhat tipsy-tursey (as the Irish would say), so be it. The Sermon on the

Mount gains its rhetorical power (as distinct from its overwhelming moral power) from anastrophe coupled with anaphora. Not the poor are blessed because and the meek are blessed because, but

> Blessed are the poor in spirit: for theirs is . . .
> Blessed are they that mourn: for they shall . . .
> Blessed are the meek: for they shall . . .

Our language is surprisingly hospitable to inversions, as in such stock phrases as "to the manner born" and "with this ring I thee wed" (a double inversion). Indulge in anastrophe with a clear conscience: you're on friendly ground.

Antimetabole: in simple inversion the sense remains unchanged—"John shouts, 'Baloney!'" and "'Baloney!' shouts John" are identical statements—whereas in antimetabole the words undergo not only a shift in position but also a change in syntax. Quintilian gives as an example:

> non ut edam vivo, sed ut vivam, edo
> [I do not live to eat, but eat to live]

and it is also true that you can take the girl out of the country but you can't take the country out of the girl.

Antithesis: pairing of contrasting words or ideas, and best when both words and ideas are contrasted.

> You write with ease, to show your breeding,
> But easy writing's vile hard reading.[3]
> It was the best of times, it was the worst of times, it was the
> age of wisdom, it was the age of foolishness, it was the epoch
> of belief, it was the epoch of incredulity, it was the season of
> Light, it was the season of Darkness, it was the spring of
> hope, it was the winter of despair, . . . [etc.][4]

Clearly, antithesis lends itself to parallel structure (discussed below). The eighteenth century, with its love of well carpentered sentences, was full of this stuff.

Apposition: placing words near other words by way of description, explanation, or amplification. Inversion is dressy:

"An avid golfer, the President was in Denver when . . ." That same structure, filled out most sumptuously, appears in the epitaph Cyrano composes for himself:

> Philosophe, physicien,
> Rimeur, bretteur, musicien,
> Et voyageur aérien,
> Grand riposteur du tic au tac,
> Amant aussi—pas pour son bien!—
> Ci-gît Hercule-Savinien
> De Cyrano de Bergerac
> Qui fut tout, et qui ne fut rien.[5]

A lot is going on in those eight short verses: alliteration, anastrophe, antithesis, apposition.

Assonance: repetition of a vowel sound in the stressed syllables of neighboring words. Willa Cather uses this device with stunning effect when she describes how two middle-aged people who had been childhood sweethearts but whose destinies had taken them in different directions for decades discover an avenue towards their spiritual junction after all:

> Whatever we had missed, we possessed together the precious, the incommunicable past.[6]

The short "e" symbolizes in sound what brings them together, what no others can share, what is to all the others expressed in a six-syllable adjective not one of whose vowels is a short "e." And by the way, do not overlook how the sentence achieves its finality through a scheme of partial rhymes—"missed . . . possessed . . . past."

Asyndeton: listing coordinate elements without using conjunctions.

> Veni, vidi, vici.
> Game, set, match!

This figure imparts a healthy forward thrust to your sentence, stirs it up, gets it moving, doesn't pause.

Chiasmus: a form of parallelism in which the second element has its main parts inverted. Take two statements of similar structure:

> I was born in this place.
> I am a native among these manners here.

Make it a single statement with a compound predicate:

> I am native here and born to the manner.

Reverse the second element and you have your chiasm:

>   . . . I am native here,
> And to the manner born.[7]

Although this looks pretty artificial, actually the figure is quite common and useful. Chiasmus is common; not common is the writer who knows its name.

Climax: arranging words, phrases, clauses, or whole sentences so that they proceed from the least important to the most important, whether in logic, eloquence, passion, or whatever. The sentences of Thoreau, Eliot, and Wilson in Chapter Three are excellent examples, dealing in phrases and clauses. A climax of single words is, perhaps, the famous plaint:

> . . . and the life of man, solitary, poor, nasty, brutish, and short.[8]

We say "perhaps," because it is not at all clear that if life is solitary, poor, nasty, and brutish we should wish it to go on forever; in such circumstances a short life may be a blessing. Logic somehow urges one to recast the sentence:

> . . . and the life of man, solitary, poor, nasty, brutish, and damned near endless.

But the original sentence has stood up for more than three centuries; why argue with success? It is pithy, concise, memorable, world-renowned, and wrongheaded.

Ellipsis: omission of word or phrase clearly implied in the context.

> What's Hecuba to him or he to Hecuba
> That he should weep for her?[9]

> What is man,
> If his chief good and market of his time
> Be but to sleep and feed? a beast, no more.[10]
> I must down to the seas again . . .[11]

Ellipsis is extremely common; sentence fragments, the norm of untutored speech, can be understood—charitably—as formal ellipses. The distinction is that stupor and sloth produce the fragment, but art and effort the ellipsis.

Epanalepsis: starting and ending a clause with the same word.

> Bone of my bones, and flesh of my flesh.[12]

Misery loves the company of misery, but pain is no cure for pain: success breeds success.

Epistrophe: using the same word or phrase at the end of successive clauses.

> For Brutus is an honorable man;
> So are they all, all honorable men . . .
> But Brutus says he was ambitious;
> And Brutus is an honorable man . . .
> Yet Brutus says he was ambitious;
> And Brutus is an honorable man . . .
> Yet Brutus says he was ambitious;
> And, sure, he is an honorable man . . .
> I should do Brutus wrong, and Cassius wrong,
> Who, you all know, are honorable men.[13]

Even on a less than Shakespearean height this is no easy figure to pull off, but it is worth keeping in mind for some special occasion when it will come in handy. You never know when something may come in handy. There was an Irish writer who had lost the use—if he ever had it—of all but the great toe of one foot, and so he typed his books with that toe, and so you see his foot came in right handy.

Hyperbaton: inversion of the normal word order. The hills among, with pleasure enough, strange though they may sound, legal they nevertheless are. Our lampoon of this figure suggests that it should be used with discretion lest it slip too quickly into mannerism, euphuism, or Gongorism. Note that we have one word that point-blank refuses to be shoved around: you cannot, you shall not, you must not say such a thing as "galore money," because galore is pure Celtic and would die the deaths if it were placed in front of the noun it is wedded to. It's money galore, and make the most of it.

Isocolon: a subspecies of parallelism, in which the parallel phrases are identical in the lengths of words used.

... government of the people, by the people, for the people ...[14]

No doubt you caught Lincoln's use of asyndeton there?

Parallelism: the statement of syntactically equivalent things in grammatically equivalent form. "Solitary, poor, nasty, brutish, and short" passes muster because all the elements are of the same ilk (adjectives); it would be a solecism to say, "solitary, poor, nasty, brutish, and a disappointment." Parallelism is one of the chief building blocks of sentences: see almost any of the sentences quoted in Chapter Three for examples. Lincoln was a devotee of this figure ("As I would not be a slave, so I would not be a master").

Parenthesis: interruption of the basic syntax in order to supply additional or even irrelevant material. Depicting Hamlet's overgushing and introverted mind, Shakespeare gives him countless parentheses, some of unusual length. The bare skeleton of the following is "Rashly . . . I groped," but see how Hamlet complicates it beyond recognition:

Hamlet.   Rashly,—
And prais'd be rashness for it; let us know

> Our indiscretion sometimes serves us well
> When our dear plots do pall; and that should teach us
> There's a divinity that shapes our ends,
> Rough-hew them how we will,—
> *Horatio.*   That is most certain.
> *Hamlet.* Up from my cabin,
> My sea-gown scarf'd about me, in the dark
> Grop'd I to find out them; had my desire . . .[15]

and so for eleven verses more, including two more instances of parenthesis ("where I found, Horatio,—O royal knavery!—an exact command . . ." and "With, ho! such bugs and goblins"). Parenthesis, syntactically, is on its own, a free agent, disconnected from the rest of the sentence and independent of it. In this it differs from apposition, in which the appositive is connected by being required to be of the same part of speech and same case as the word to which it stands in apposition.

Polyptoton: repetition of a word-root in varied forms, as, to think the unthinkable, or:

> Then had I not been thus exiled from light;
> As in the land of darkness yet in light,
> To live a life half dead, a living death,
> And buried; but O yet more miserable!
> Myself, my sepulcher, a moving grave,
> Buried, yet not exempt
> By privilege of death and burial . . .[16]

We count ten figures (including some figures used more than once) in those few verses. Slow down: densely populated.

Polysyndeton: the opposite of asyndeton, this figure indulges in conjunctions galore:

> And God blessed Noah and his sons, and said unto them, Be fruitful, and multiply, and replenish the earth. And the fear of you and the dread of you shall be upon every beast of the earth, and upon every fowl of the air, upon all that moveth upon the earth, and upon all the fishes of the sea . . . [17]

In "The Tyger," one of the poetic peaks in our language, Blake actually makes use of the contrast between polysyndeton and asyndeton in consecutive stanzas. Polysyndeton with its repeated connectives tends to impart a stately movement, but as the emotion rises and the fever takes hold, Blake drops all connectives:

> And what shoulder, & what art,
> Could twist the sinews of thy heart?
> And when thy heart began to beat,
> What dread hand? & what dread feet?
>
> What the hammer? what the chain?
> In what furnace was thy brain?
> What the anvil? what dread grasp
> Dare its deadly terrors clasp?[18]

A moment of inspection will show you that you can rewrite the second stanza using a bunch of connectives if you wish. Blake knew that: he omitted them for a definite reason. He done right.

Tropes

Allegory: any extended metaphor (admittedly a simple definition: on this matter the rhetoricians go bonkers and have a lovely time). You make a metaphor when you say man is an animal. George Orwell extended the idea to the length of a novella and produced *Animal Farm*.

Antanaclasis: repetition of a word but in a different sense.

> We must indeed all hang together, or, most assuredly, we shall all hang separately.[19]

Anthimeria: use of a word that is normally one part of speech in a situation that requires it to be understood as a different part of speech. In English, and this is one of its greatest virtues, almost any noun can be verbed. Indeed, one can read scarce a page of Shakespeare without running across some new verb hatched out of his teeming loin. "To scarf," for example, was the verb implied in Hamlet's speech just above, where he says, "My sea-gown scarf'd about me." But he will create a verb from an adjective when the spirit moves:

> And thus the native hue of resolution
> Is sicklied o'er with the pale cast of thought . . .[20]

So Shakespeare around 1600. Strangely, *Webster's Ninth New Collegiate* finds no written use of "to sickly" before 1763. Webster isn't what it used to be.

Antonomasia: substitution of a title, class-name, or epithet for a proper name, or vice versa—"the brass" for General So-and-So, or "Horowitz" for pianist. More innocent than periphrasis, which see.

Apostrophe: addressing an absent person or a personified abstraction.

> Milton! thou shouldst be living at this hour:
> England hath need of thee: she is a fen . . .[21]
> O death, where is thy sting? O grave, where is thy victory?[22]

Auxesis: puffing something up by calling it a seriouser name than it deserves. Mr. Bush's "New World Order" is an instance of auxesis aggravated by historical amnesia. Puff something up until it explodes in your face and you have hyperbole, which see.

Erotema: a "rhetorical question," asked not to elicit a reply but to suggest or assert something:

> Hath not a Jew eyes? Hath not a Jew hands, organs, dimensions, senses, affections, passions? Fed with the same food, hurt with the same weapons, subject to the same diseases, heal'd by the same means, warm'd and cool'd by the same winter and summer, as a Christian is? If you prick us, do we not bleed? If you tickle us, do we not laugh? If you poison us, do we not die? And if you wrong us, shall we not revenge?[23]

Much of that scans nicely as blank verse, by the bye.

Hyperbole: exaggeration, usually exaggerated, to produce certain effects. Mr. Nixon signed a document in 1971 and called it the most important monetary event in history (does anyone recall what it was?). P. T. Barnum ran "The Greatest Show On Earth." Mr. Johnson stirred the breezes with his "Great Society." Hyperbole seems a ready breeding ground for advertising men and political adventurers—reason enough, right there, to avoid it pretty consistently. Nay, squash it with your foot and throw it to the wolves.

Irony: using a word to express the opposite of its literal meaning; disapproval masquerading as praise.

> For Brutus is an honorable man.[13]

> (of Ever-Ever Land i speak
> sweet morons gather roun'
> who does not dare to stand or sit
> may take it lying down)[24]

Litotes: affirming something by negating its opposite. He's no slouch; she wasn't born yesterday; this is no laughing matter.

> But Paul said, I am a man which am a Jew of Tarsus, a city in Cilicia, a citizen of no mean city . . .[25]

Litotes is a form of understatement, characterized by the negative statement. Direct understatement—"New York is a busy town"— needs no comment, no encyclopaedic disquisition.

Meiosis: understatement pure and simple.

> We are na fou, we're nae that fou,
> But just a drappie in our ee.[26]

Metaphor: departing from literal meaning in order to suggest a likeness. He was a pig at the table; Liszt could make the piano thunder; Justice is blind; she was an angel; was Richard really lion-hearted?

> Much have I travel'd in the realms of gold,
> And many goodly states and kingdoms seen . . .[27]

Keats sustains the travel metaphor throughout his sonnet, abiding by the law that says Thou Shalt Not Mix 'Em. Your words may rush like a torrent and your arguments may break into little pieces on the hard heads of your audience, but you cannot say your torrent of words broke into little pieces, etc. Almost all words are metaphorical in themselves, thanks to their derivation from concrete terms; which is to say that metaphor is *the* fundamental spirit of language and communication (if you have never seen a zebra but do know about horses first-hand, then I can describe a zebra to you by talking about a horse). So the first place to start in sprucing up your writing style is metaphor: think metaphor, write metaphor, live it.

Metonymy: naming a thing by naming an attribute or accompaniment of it. Town & gown, the distaff side, bottle baby, flattop, Ivy League, silver screen, mailed fist, sawbones, chicken & mashed potatoes circuit, shrink.

Onomatopoeia: a word whose pronunciation mimics the sound of the thing named. Buzz, murmur, babble, swish, gobbledygook, lallapalooza.

> A needless Alexandrine ends the song,
> That, like a wounded snake, drags its slow length along.[28]

There is great freedom of invention in this figure. You can screech and howl to your heart's content.

Oxymoron: union in syntax of terms that clash in logic—a warring union, a joined disjunction, a reasoned madness, a lovely nuisance, a sober senator. Milton's "darkness visible" is among the most illustrious instances of this fine and startling figure.

Parable: a story, which may or may not be true, told to point up a moral; differs from allegory, which is understood to be fanciful (but not frivolous: it, too, teaches). Perhaps the headwaters of this pleasing figure are the parables of Jesus and the fables of Aesop.

Paradox: like oxymoron, paradox involves the collision of contradictory items, but this time not individual words but whole phrases, clauses, concepts. Because the order of the words is not important, paradox is not a Scheme; and yet it is a figure; and so by eliminating all other choices we may call it a Trope, though none too proudly. A man never stands so tall as when he bends down to help a child. *Festina lente.*

> He that findeth his life shall lose it: and he that loseth his life for my sake shall find it.[29]

It is a paradox that writers of paradox are mainly dogmatists. Or is it?

Paralipsis: a form of irony in which one gets one's message across by suggesting the outlines of the message that one is struggling to suppress. We are not going to say that paralipsis is a form of cowardice, no, nor that it is a form of deception. On that matter our lips are sealed. Nor is it incumbent upon us to mention that paralipsis is the habitual refuge of the courtroom mechanic, who abuses it in order to suggest to the jury what he can very well deny to the judge ever having said. Nor will we . . .

Paronomasia: a play on words that sound the same but are spelt differently. A pun. Don't. (However, see Chapter Four for the kind of pun that may perhaps pass muster.)

Periphrasis: roundabout way of talking. Differs from antonomasia in that periphrasis is the camouflage of him who sets out to deceive or befuddle or smudge. Revolution? Nothing of the kind, sir. A few of the boys gathered at Boston Harbor the other evening and had a tea party, in some quantity, for they are lads of high humor, you know, sir, and . . .

Personification: attributing human qualities or abilities to objects or abstractions. The gardens prayed for rain; the birds sought solace in the shadows; the proud cat lorded it over the barn; Congress governed.

Prosopopoeia: representing the speech or action of an absent or imaginary person.

'What are the bugles blowin' for?' said Files-on-Parade.
'To turn you out, to turn you out,' the Colour-Sergeant
   said.'[30]

East is personification, prosopopoeia west, and never the twain
shall meet.

Pun: a play on words. There are three types: antanaclasis
(see above), syllepsis (see below), and paronomasia (don't).

Rhetorical question: erotema (which see). Is this not a wild
goose chase?

Simile: saying that one thing is like another (whereas metaphor
says one thing actually is another).

John Anderson my jo, John,
   When we were first acquent,
Your locks were like the raven,
   Your bonie brow was brent;
But now your brow is beld, John,
   Your locks are like the snaw;
But blessings on your frosty pow,
   John Anderson my jo![31]

Note how the parallelism of the similes contributes to the struc-
tural soundness of the stanza. Note, also, the metaphor, "frosty,"
to be understood, in this context, as white, not frigid (one fondly
hopes).

Syllepsis: use of one word in relation to two or more other
words with the result that it changes its meaning in each instance.

Those heads, as stomachs, are not sure the best,
Which nauseate all, and nothing can digest.[32]

In which the basic structure includes "those heads [and] stomachs
which nauseate . . ." Note how this differs from Franklin's antanaclasis on hanging.

Synecdoche: letting a part stand for the whole. As, somewhat loosely, genus for species: animal for horse. Or species for
genus: Give us this day our daily bread. Or, more strictly, part for

whole: "Friends, Romans, countrymen, lend me your ears!"[13] Or, finally, raw material for object made from it: flesh and bone for body or person, gold for money or riches, tongue for speech.

Zeugma: one term syntactically governing two or more others, with grammatical or logical relation to only one of them. Leading to such sticky wickets as, "the authority and protection which a parent exercises . . ." When there is no flaw, but the one word must undergo a slight shift in meaning in order to make sense, there is opportunity for wit, as when the debauched secretary of the Navy, Lord Sandwich, said to the rectitudinous reformer John Wilkes, "You will die on the gallows or of the pox," and Wilkes replied, "That depends, my lord, on whether I embrace your policies or your mistress."

CHAPTER SIX

Persuade Your Reader

R HETORIC, "the art of effective speaking," as it was first defined about 2,500 years ago, includes more than one form of effectiveness. You may set yourself the task of amusing your audience; you may wish to touch their emotions; you may need to persuade them of something. Of the first two types we have pretty well covered the waterfront in earlier chapters; in this one let's have a go at persuasion, the art thereof.*

The downfall of a tyrant brought the rise of rhetoric. Thrasybulus of Syracuse was deposed sometime in the first third of the fifth century B.C., and democracy, more or less, replaced the tyrant. The citizens of Syracuse, making use of their new freedom, sued in the courts to regain title to their hereditary lands and estates. One Corax of Syracuse, noting that these amateur petitioners were botching their cases, published in 466 B.C. a how-to book, *Techne Logon* ("the art of words"), which is the earliest known formulation of rhetorical principles. That work has been lost, but some goodly part of the systems fashioned by Corax and his pupil, Tisias, can be gleaned from scattered references in the work of later thinkers—Plato, Aristotle, Cicero, Quintilian. Perhaps it is enough, for our purpose, to mention that Corax listed the divisions that became traditional in the oratory of our civilization: proem, narration, arguments (both confirming one's position and

---

*NB: This section owes its structure and much of its argument (but none of its prose) to Edward P. J. Corbett, *Classical Rhetoric for the Modern Student* (New York: Oxford University Press, 1971).

refuting one's opponent), subsidiary remarks, and peroration. There you have the *structure* of your persuasive utterance (whether spoken or written).

Proem and narration, arising as they do from the specific elements of each case, offer no rhetorical difficulty. It is in the argument that you may find you need a systematic approach, and that is exactly what the ancients have designed for you. In searching for argument in support of your cause, you can run through the "places" ("Topics" is the rhetorical term) where arguments are to be found. The classical rhetoric identifies five Topics: *definition, comparison, relationship, circumstance,* and *testimony.* We propose to have a look at these beasties.

Definition

This does not mean the schoolboy's passing the buck by saying, "Webster defines so-and-so as . . ." No: the task is to define, to delimit, a particular situation or claim, not a generality such as the common denotation of a linguistic term. What is at stake? What is the deep and genuine issue before us? What are its limits? Definition proceeds along two main avenues: genus and division.

Definition by genus sounds ivory tower enough, but it can be in dead earnest. In the matter of abortion, for example, everything hangs on the definition of the creature subject to abortion: if we define it as a human being, then we condemn abortion as premeditated manslaughter; if we define it as something not human, we can shift the ground of discourse to a question of freedom of choice.

Definition by division allows your argument to proceed in bite-sized pieces. You may define a claim to landed property as being legal if it arises from conquest (in olden time), purchase, inheritance, marriage, or contract (as in the settlement of a gambling debt). You can show the court in Syracuse that none but you can make some such claim to a given property, and so on.

Similarly, you can divide an element into its component features. Once again, in the matter of abortion you can define a human being as possessing the following characteristics and abilities—A, B, C, D, E—and then you can show that the embryo at the moment of conception possesses none of these; therefore, it is not human. The counterdefinition observes that the embryo at the moment of conception possesses its complete lifetime supply of genetic material and information and is, genetically speaking, a perfected and independent creature that is as human as it can be.

Comparison

We've mentioned that metaphor is at the very core of language; our minds naturally seek out and express what similarities they find among different objects. Under the general head of comparison you may find arguments based on similarity, difference, and degree.

Similarity and *difference* account for a large part of legal reasoning, as the law is an accumulation of decisions and rulings in cases that have already gone into the books. One side can argue that the current case is similar to a certain older case and therefore deserves a similar decision. The other side can argue that the cases contain subtle but decisive differences, and so the current case cannot be controlled by the earlier ruling. Military and political decisions proceed by such arguments: no two campaigns are the same, and yet there are similarities (terrain, climate, logistics, human resources) and differences (matériel, timing, numbers). If you argue similarities between things of different orders, as you usually must do in human affairs, you will be arguing by analogy, which, though it seldom constitutes proof, yet suggests at least some cogency in your position.

Degree, the more or less of similar or identical things, provides many familiar forms of argument, all neatly placed in cubbyholes by that inveterate gatherer and classifier, Aristotle. He said that a greater number of things (if desirable in themselves) is preferable to a smaller number. "The more the merrier!" He said that a means to an end is less desirable than the end itself. He said the rare is more precious than the commonplace. He said that the ignorant will prefer less worthy things than men of practical wisdom (a form of the appeal to authority, to be discussed under "Testimony"). He said the exact opposite in the next breath: the majority will choose something better than the minority (he assumed that the masses choose what is immediately desirable, and so that is best which appeals to the most—a variation of the "forty million Frenchmen can't be wrong" argument). He said that what men desire deep down is a greater good than what they are content to merely seem to possess; health is therefore a greater value than justice, because men are happy if they are merely reputed to be just, but they'd rather enjoy real health than just seem to be healthy. He said that if a thing doesn't exist in a likely place, it is not to be found in a less likely place—the *a fortiori* argument (in the matter of abortion, we encounter it in this form: if they kill defenseless infants, is there anyone in this society who can expect mercy? to which the counterthrust, admittedly hyperbolic, runs something like this: if a woman can't exercise freedom of choice within her own body, is freedom safe anywhere in this society?). It is illuminating to observe that on abortion, a question of high current interest, everyone has an opinion usually vociferous and passionate, and involving medical and legal and social aspects thoroughly up to date, and yet nobody on either side has come forth with an argument that is not some form or combination of the rhetorical avenues first laid out twenty-five centuries ago.

Relationship

The general topic of relationship may be divided into four parts: cause and effect, antecedent and consequence, contraries, and contradictions.

Cause and effect, one of the most basic forms of reasoning, requires no small degree of circumspection. To assign a cause and make it stick, you must be prepared to show that the cause is sufficient to produce the effect; that it is the most likely cause among several possible causes; that the conditions do not inhibit the cause from working its effect; and that the cause invariably produces the effect. (In such muddy waters as statecraft and social policy, "invariably" gives way to "with a high degree of probability.") Note that it is not enough to show that one thing always follows another: the streets are dry, and then it rains and the streets are wet; then they dry out and it rains again and once again they are wet; does this prove that dry streets cause rain?

Antecedent and consequence is a less rigorous form of the cause and effect argument. The dry climate of the Sonora Desert has attracted a disproportionate number of people who suffer from tuberculosis. If you have a dry climate, you will play host to a crowd of valetudinarians, but that doesn't mean that Arizona's climate causes tuberculosis. For purposes of analysis it is useful to remember that most antecedent–consequence arguments can be rephrased as syllogisms if you supply the missing term (the hidden assumption). Getting back to the glorious Southwest: 1) Dry climates attract tuberculars; 2) Arizona has a dry climate; therefore 3) Arizona has a lot of tuberculars.

Contraries differ from difference. Difference occurs between items of different orders, contraries between items of the same order. Liberty and bondage are contraries in the general order of external restraint on human action. Liberty, a political good, differs from license, a moral failing, but is not contrary to it. Contraries offer an avenue of proof in certain cases: since two contraries cannot both be true, you can prove one to be false if you prove the other to be true. But proving one contrary to be false doesn't do the job, because both contraries can be false; you must still prove the other one true. Proving Sally's not a blonde doesn't prove she's a brunette; she could be a redhead.

Contradictions are mutually exclusive, and one of them must be true and the other false (the candle is burning; it is not burning); whereas contraries permit weaseling (the candle is burning; it is flickering). If you can spy a chance to set up a pair of contradictories, by all means do so: they put starch into the argument every time.

Circumstance

The two main lines of discourse under the general head of circumstance are the possible and the impossible, and past fact and future fact.

The possible and the impossible comes in six Aristotelian flavors. If one of a pair of *contraries* is possible, then the other is possible (if bondage is possible, so is liberty). If one of a pair of *similar* items is possible, so is the other (if you can swim the crawl, you can swim the backstroke). If a *difficult* thing is possible, then an easier one is (if you can recite the alphabet backwards . . .). A *beginning* implies a *conclusion*, and vice versa (what is possible can be begun; what is impossible, never: there is no such thing as the first step in the proof that two plus two equals five). If the *parts* are possible, so is the whole, and vice versa (if we had some ham we could have ham and eggs, if we had some eggs). If a thing is possible without *special* exertions, surely it is possible with preparation and planning (if a child can learn his native language, surely a scholar can).

Past fact, the question whether something has happened or not, is useful in establishing precedent. *Future fact*, the question whether a certain event or situation is likely to be encountered in the future, is an important element in weighing various courses of action.

What can be said about past fact hews closely to common sense. If a rare event has occurred, a similar but more common event has probably also occurred (he hit a homer that day; he probably got on base a couple of times too). If two events are closely associated and one of them has happened, the other has happened as well (Socrates, according to legend, returning home after an all-night symposium with the boys, is greeted by Xanthippe, who gives him a loud tongue-lashing and then upends the chamber pot on his head, whereupon he says, "After all that thunder, I knew I should expect rain"). If someone had the motive, the means, and the opportunity to do something, he probably did do it (cf. Agatha Christie and her sisters). With reverse English these arguments can be used to deny the likelihood of a past fact.

As for future fact: if motive and means are present, a certain deed will probably take place; if antecedents are here, consequences will follow (when youngsters get married, they will probably have children); if the means to a particular end are available, and if that end is desired, then the means will probably be put to use and the end attained (tax revenues are the means whereby a corrupt democracy maintains itself in power; any increase in tax revenues causes an increase in spending).

Testimony

The last of the major Topics is testimony, which may be discussed under six subheads: authority, testimonial, statistics, maxims, law, and precedent. And then we shall indulge in a few general remarks.

Authority, some say, isn't what it used to be: in some mythical past the common run of people accepted unblinkingly whatever the Authorities told them, whereas in this "modern," "scientific," "democratic" age your Man In The Street looks at everything with a keenly skeptical eye and a mind all geared to tolerate nothing less than laboratory precision and mathematical elegance for proof. How this heaven of intellectual rigor and probity has opened up at the very time when every survey of

American educational attainment places us somewhere near the bottom of the heap no one has paused to explain, perhaps because no one has bothered himself to ask. No, a New Age of Human Intelligence has not dawned: the old Authorities, most of them, have simply been shunted aside, with the snide remarks usually reserved for the defenseless, and have been replaced by new Authorities, whose word is accepted just as unblinkingly as that of the old. Something there is in the human heart that craves Authority but becomes restless with any one Authority too long in the saddle. So the Authorities today are opinion surveyors, television news dictators old enough to sport a few grey hairs and look serious, popular theatrical stars doubling in brass and giving pomposity a bad name, retired athletes, and academic scientists whose magisterial Authority somehow fails to see something a little funny in a marine biologist's hogging the national broadcast waves to prattle on and on about military strategy or women's rights in Timbuktu. The point is that you can still make the classical appeal to Authority but only if you invoke an Authority that your audience accepts. And today, just as two millennia ago, think twice before you mention an Authority who has given contradictory testimony in the past, who is known to hold some prejudice that may color his witness, who may have a chip on his shoulder or a pet peeve or a pet project, who may be basing his conclusions on work that has gone stale when there is fresher evidence to consult, who is a maverick (like that wonderful MIT professor who announced that the "yellow rain" attacks of airborne poison in Indochina were really the work of swarms of bees on their vernal defecation flight after a long winter of constipation).

Testimonials come in a jillion forms, all of them having the feature that they quote the opinion of someone other than yourself, someone with no personal stake in your cause. Opinion surveys, market research data, endorsements, all these can be cited as testimonials. But testimonials do not constitute proof; they are an appeal not to reason, but to the ethical sense; and so they can be knocked into a cocked hat all too easily.

Statistics, as everybody knows, called forth one of Mark Twain's sharpest barbs. To the extent that statistics are merely an arithmetical way of laying out the findings of an opinion survey, they are testimonials with the characteristic weaknesses of polling processes: faulty sample, skewed questions, unwarranted assumptions (that everyone does know his opinion on a given issue, and that he will be willing to offer it to a stranger). To the extent that statistics are something other than opinion malls, they require intense scrutiny before you buy any given interpretation of them. We have already mentioned that statistical datum about the incidence of tuberculosis in Arizona; that was a prime sample of a statistic that could not be swallowed whole except by a certified fool. Another sample, not too shopworn one hopes, is the statement that a man can drown in a river whose average depth is only one inch (one wonders if that is the Powder River in Wyoming, "a mile wide and an inch deep, too thin to plow and too thick to drink"). Figures on economic growth (or decline) appear to be accurate and have the sanction of mathematical and statistical science, and yet the very basis of every statistical statement on growth is completely arbitrary and capricious: the fellow setting up the framework of measurement selects the starting year, and he can select it to serve his own purposes, and 87.3 per cent of the time he will. (Where did that figure come from? We made it up!) The statistics brought into play in discussions of government finance are horrible examples of willful distortion through canny selection of starting points, finishing points, and other definitional niceties. It is almost impossible to use statistical arguments when discussing the taxation of personal incomes, because the tax law makes such excruciatingly difficult problems of definition that there is no general agreement, for example, on whether wealth is measured as income or assets, whether capital enhancement is measured as ordinary income, whether an expense is normal or reasonable, and so on through fifty thousand pages of the current year's rules and regulations. Moral: if you use statistics, be sure to understand exactly what they say and imply, and make sure you spell it all out ahead of time. And if your opposite number uses them, rip him to pieces.

Maxims embody the accumulated wisdom of the tribe, "What oft was thought but ne'er so well expressed." They are a form of the appeal to Authority, this time to the authority of our now anonymous ancestors. Maxims gain authority when we contemplate that they are the wisdom of the generations who survived a hundred hard centuries and learned the secrets of living and passed those secrets along, thanks to which we are alive today. The trouble with maxims, however, is that life is paradoxical and sometimes downright unfathomable, so that the wisdom of the tribe contains many sayings and proverbs that cancel each other out. "Penny wise and pound foolish" does constant battle with "A dollar saved is a dollar earned." "He who hesitates is lost" may play second fiddle to "Look before you leap." "Faith moves mountains" has a score to settle with "God helps those who help themselves." Maxims—listen to Sancho Panza!—are fun, but if you haul them into any serious attempt at argumentation, be prepared for the countermaxim.

Law, in this context, comprises any documentary or contractual or statutory evidence that can be dragged in by the heels to support your argument. But a piece of paper with script or printing on it is a scrap of paper and nothing more if your opposite number can show that there is no connection between the document and the supposed writer of same, or if the document was signed in the absence of witnesses, or if the document is not the original but only a copy, or if the document is worded differently from the original, or if there are no people to protest the authenticity of the document (using "protest" in the old sense), or if the document is superseded by another. These questions are not idle. Huge hot controversies eddy about the authenticity of documents. Think of the "Heiligenstadt Testament" of Beethoven, the so-called "Protocols of the Elders of Zion," or the so-called "Pumpkin Papers" (actually microfilms) that figured so importantly in the Hiss-Chambers case. By all means, summon documents to your service, but take pains that they be signed in blood and witnessed by three Supreme Court Justices.

Precedent is, strictly speaking, a child of courtroom argumentation. It is useful in law because the already decided case exists within the limits described by the evidence and testimony of record; a current suit can be stepped off against it to see how it measures up. Not so in "real life," where the contingencies and circumstances of one case are beyond number, and where it is taken for granted that every situation is unique. This is self-evident: old folks always say the world "isn't what it used to be when I was young," and what they mean is that it would be impossible to duplicate the circumstances of their youth. In real life there are no precedents. In law there sometimes are. Real life costs less and is more fun.

Some General Remarks

In your effort to write (or speak) persuasively, pay attention to the requirement that you make yourself acceptable to your audience. You are a performer, after all: and even Horowitz would put his feet together, hang his fabled hands down at his sides, and bow his head to his audience. Start out by some note of ingratiation. Move to the business at hand by mentioning that there is a dispute of some sort. Give full and utterly fair-minded statement to the position of the other party (this is extremely important: it shows the audience that you have taken the trouble to examine the question under discussion, and it forces you to understand exactly what you are up against).

Move, then, into your arguments (which the Topics will have suggested to you). Lay it all out clean and fair. Once done with that, you can sum up the debate and then move to your peroration, which—if anywhere—is the place for you to pull out the stops and either move them to salty tears or bring them to their feet.

Wait for the tumult to subside, and then don't forget to give them Godspeed.

APPENDIX A

Book Notes

T HERE ARE shelvesful of reference works and usage guides on the market. Of the good ones, some are known to every experienced writer; others are unjustly obscure. Herewith, a highly selective bibliographical catalogue.

MANUALS OF STYLE

Books on writing and style may be divided into three general categories: 1) usage guides, literary; 2) usage guides, nuts & bolts; 3) how-to-write books.

Usage Guides, Literary

The granddaddy of them all (to use our native idiom, which was shoved aside for a while by Saddam Hussein's mother) is Fowler: that is, *Modern English Usage*, by H. W. Fowler (Oxford: Clarendon Press, 1926). In the Fifties and Sixties Oxford published two quite different updatings of this book*—*Fowler's Modern English Usage*, revised by Sir Ernest Gowers (Oxford: Clarendon Press, 1965), and *A Dictionary of American-English Usage, based on Fowler's Modern English Usage*, by Margaret Nicholson (New York: Oxford

---

*Not to be confused with the many reprintings of the first edition, in this country as well as in Britain, up into the early 1950s.

University Press, 1957)—but we recommend the original version. And we recommend it not as an antiquarian curiosity but as the most useful guide there is to this wonderful, exasperating language of ours.

To be sure, some of Fowler's specific advice—especially on matters of punctuation and pronunciation—no longer applies. What was "modern English usage" in the 1920s is not always modern American usage in the 1990s. But most of Fowler's work survives the passage of time, because he is a teacher, not a dictator. He doesn't just tell us, for example: Use the subjunctive here; avoid it there. Instead, he explains how usage of the subjunctive has evolved, thus giving us a way of judging where matters stand in our own day. In entries such as the one where he distinguishes among *essential*, *necessary*, and *requisite*, he not only helps us grasp the shades of meaning of these particular words but, while he's at it, shows us how to analyze any pair or group of abstract words. Even on so small a matter as whether to say *emulatable* or *emulable*, he makes his reasoning clear.

We have referred to Fowler throughout on specific matters of style; here is a sample of his own style, concluding the entry on Mannerism:

> Perhaps few of those who write much escape from the temptation to trade on tricks of which they have learnt the effectiveness; & it is true that it is a delicate matter to discern where a peculiarity ceases to be an element in the individuality that readers associate pleasantly with the writer they like, & becomes a recurrent & looked-for & dreaded irritation. But at least it is well for every writer to realize that, for his as for other people's mannerisms, there is a point at which that transformation does take place.

Next on our list is *Modern American Usage*, by Wilson Follett, edited and completed by Jacques Barzun, in collaboration with Carlos Baker, Frederick W. Dupee, Dudley Fitts, James D. Hart, Phyllis McGinley, and Lionel Trilling (New York: Warner Paperback Library, 1966). Like Fowler, this work is in dictionary form, with the entries ranging from a few lines to several pages. Also like Fowler, it is quirky and individual. That galaxy of Columbia professors who undertook to complete Professor Follett's work after his death kept their own personalities out of the way.

Much of Follett's advice is sound, and he too lays out his reasoning in such a way that the reader can decide whether it is still applicable. The article SHALL (SHOULD)/WILL (WOULD) is a masterly (but not, as Follett points out elsewhere, masterful) piece of grammatical untangling.

A distant third among the comprehensive guides is *A Dictionary of Contemporary American Usage*, by Bergen Evans and Cornelia Evans (New York: Random House, 1957). It begins with the amazing revelation that "a and an are two forms of the same word" and goes on from there. Most of its individual entries—distinguishing between similar words; tracing common expressions to their origins (usually for the purpose of rejecting them as clichés)—are competent, and many are interesting; but it is hard to place any confidence in grammarians who assert: "In American English *shall* is always a present subjunctive. . . ."

There is a constant stream of other, far less comprehensive usage books—many of them entertaining, though none a substitute for Fowler and Follett.

Theodore Bernstein, for decades an editor at *The New York Times*, produced an occasional newsletter called *Winners & Sinners* in which he pointed out grammatical errors *Times* writers had submitted, laid down the law about usages he disapproved of, applauded brilliant stories and headlines, and gave entertaining samples of what happens when an editor falls asleep at the switch—e.g., "Meet Mr. Sea. 'Nicely acted throughout by a shipshape little cast, featuring Sterling Hayden in the title role . . .' The title of the picture: 'The Eternal Sea.'"* Bernstein produced several

---

Miss Thistlebottom's Hobgoblins, p. 185.

books based on *Winners & Sinners*, including *The Careful Writer: A Modern Guide to English Usage* (New York: Atheneum, 1965) and *Miss Thistlebottom's Hobgoblins: The Careful Writer's Guide to the Taboos, Bugbears, and Outmoded Rules of English Usage* (New York: Farrar, Straus, 1971). We often disagree with Bernstein, but many editors swear by him.

Ubiquitous nowadays are William Safire's collections of his weekly *New York Times Magazine* columns—including *On Language* (New York: Times Books, 1980), *Take My Word for It* (New York: Henry Holt, 1987), and *The Language Maven Strikes Again* (New York: Doubleday, 1990). If you like the Safire style—"Some Thistlebottom, whose marbles are all puries, is taking leaky pen in hand at this moment to write a complaint about 'commentate,' a clip used here to mean 'making analytical noises like a commentator'"*—you will like these; otherwise, otherwise.

Then there is our colleague John Simon, whose language columns for *Esquire* and *More* magazines yielded *Paradigms Lost* (New York: Clarkson N. Potter, 1980). Simon is no gentler with erring writers than he is with pandering directors and ham actors: "I immediately asked Stein whether [Tennessee] Williams had actually said 'between he and I,' and Harry solemnly confirmed the melancholy fact. The man who after Eugene O'Neill was our best playwright—I say *was* because his later plays have been pitiful travesties of his beautiful early ones—had committed a grammatical error of *unsurpassable* grossness" (p. 18). Fortunately for this book, there is more good work done in print than in film, and pieces such as Simon's review of Eric Partridge's *A Dictionary of Catch Phrases*, or his account of working with Jacques Barzun, Lionel Trilling, and W. H. Auden on *The Mid-Century*, provide relief from the battle.

A battler from a previous generation who is well worth hunting up is A. P. Herbert. The subtitle of his *What a Word!*

---

*On Language, p. 22.

(London: Methuen, 1935) gives the flavor: *Being an Account of the Principles & Progress of 'The Word War' conducted in 'Punch,' to the great Improvement and Delight of the People, and the lasting Benefit of the King's English, with many Ingenious Exercises and Horrible Examples.* Herbert's method is to consider the implications of a dubious coinage so exuberantly that you can never again meet the word or phrase without chortling:

> Cannot the advertiser see that an advertisement based upon a ridiculously wrong or meaningless word is like a great car with a flat tyre? 'exceptional acceleration and hill-climbing, improved roadability, smoother running and lower fuel consumption.' What sort of car, I wonder, is a car which is not 'roadable'? Is it a 'hedgeable' or 'ditchable' or perhaps a 'turfable' car? Does it leap fences but refuse to travel on roads? Does it achieve high velocity in bogs or ploughed fields but show unstartability in Oxford Street? . . . [p. 51].

Usage Guides, Nuts & Bolts

In this category are the stylebooks of major publishing enterprises, produced for the organizations' writers and editors but offered to the general public as well. Since a newspaper or magazine doesn't want five different spellings of the same word tripping through its pages, it chooses one and makes it official, even if another spelling might be equally good. Book publishers also have a house style, although they allow more variety from one book to another than periodicals allow from one article to another.

Stylebooks are catalogues of these choices; as such they can be of great use to the student or the professional writer, relieving him of the task of reinventing the wheel. However, they are not concerned to teach, as Fowler and Follett are, and therefore are less helpful to the general reader.

The most comprehensive Nuts & Bolts stylebooks come from book publishers. For general use, *The Chicago Manual of Style*

(Chicago: University of Chicago Press, 1982) is regarded as the standard. It covers everything from the use of the comma in apposition, to the proper form for the copyright notice, to lists of abbreviations, to word division in foreign languages. *The Chicago Manual*—now in its 13th edition—is seldom lively, but it is thorough.

The McGraw-Hill Style Manual: A Concise Guide for Writers and Editors, edited by Marie Longyear (New York: McGraw-Hill, 1989), is particularly strong on scientific and mathematical orthography; it also offers a general section on usage, drawing frequently on Fowler and Follett. Our times being what they are, it has a lengthy chapter on "Bias-Free Publishing"; this is saner than most such disquisitions, containing, for example, this paragraph:

> Many people believe that the English language itself does much to shape attitudes and have suggested that the word *man* and the male pronoun *he, him*, and *his* be replaced in all generic senses. Whether such a radical change in the vernacular can ever be accomplished by willing it so is open to question. But wherever you stand on this issue, you should be aware that the people responsible for purchasing textbooks (adoption committees, administrators, and teachers) will generally reject a text that inadvertently uses sexist language [p. 279].

There are plenty of other Nuts & Bolts guides around—notably *The New York Times Manual of Style and Usage*, edited by Lewis Jordan (New York: Times Books, 1976) and *The Associated Press Stylebook and Libel Manual*, edited by Christopher W. French, Eileen Alt Powell, and Howard Angione (Reading, Mass.: Addison-Wesley, 1982)—but compared to *The Chicago Manual* and *The McGraw-Hill Style Manual*, these seem skimpy and not especially useful to anyone not employed by the issuing organization.

How-to-Write Books

The best known, by a mile, is Strunk & White: *The Elements of*

Style, by William Strunk, Jr., with Revisions, an Introduction, and a New Chapter on Writing, by E. B. White (New York: Macmillan Paperbacks, 1959). Although *The Elements of Style* is widely used in freshman composition classes, it is not really a *teaching* work, helping the reader, as Fowler and Follett do, to see more clearly how the English language works. Instead, it is a list of rules, most of them in the imperative mood, some elaborated at length, others not. Although we have taken more than one swipe at Strunk & White for their keep-it-simple credo, the book is useful—as a starting point. If more people followed Strunk's rules, we would not have seas of bureaucratic prose to drown in; if everyone did, the world of English prose would be a dull place. White notes that Abraham Lincoln was "flirting with disaster" when he said: "Four score and seven years ago," though White winds up approving of the elevated language; present-day computer programs that correct your grammar, we hear,* flunk Mr. Lincoln out of hand: "Grammatik pounces on Abraham Lincoln for saying, 'Now we *are engaged* in a great civil war,' scolding him for using the passive voice which the software dislikes. . . . On an index of the strength of delivery, [RightWriter] rates the Gettysburg Address an even zero, indicating 'a weak, wordy writing style.'"

Professor Strunk's favorite phrase, Mr. White tells us, was "Omit needless words" (Rule #13). Strunk himself omitted words so relentlessly that he had to say everything three times to make up the full hour of class. But at least when he gives examples of words to omit, they mostly *are* needless. Rudolf Flesch—whether writing alone in *The Art of Readable Writing* (New York: Harper & Brothers, 1949) or with A. H. Lass in the current paperback *A New Guide to Better Writing* (New York: Warner Books, 1979)—doesn't stop at fat; he cuts right through to living muscle and bone. "The furniture was full of decorations that had been painted by hand" is indeed, as Flesch & Lass tell us, just a clumsy way of saying,

---

*Computer Software for Writers: Helping the Bad, Hurting the Good?" by David Wessel, *The Wall Street Journal* (July 7, 1986).

"The furniture was full of hand-painted decorations." But "He covered the two miles with a speed that amazed everybody" may say more than "He covered the two miles with amazing speed," and "Often the beauty of a dress lies in the wearing" is not as clear as "Often the beauty of a dress lies in the way it is worn."

Reading Flesch, we are reminded of the Fresh Fish story. The fishmonger Klotnick has acquired a nice piece of wood to use as a sign, but he isn't sure it is big enough for what he wants to say: Fresh Fish Sold Here Daily. Just then his friend Rubinstein comes along, and Klotnick asks for his advice. Well, says Rubinstein, you don't want to say *Fresh*—that'll set people wondering if the fish maybe aren't so fresh. And you don't need *Sold*—would you give them away? *Here* is a mistake—where else would you sell them? And *Daily* you don't need—if the shop's open, you're selling. Come to think of it, the people can see the fish in the window—so why bother with *Fish*?

That way lies silence—which is golden only if you have nothing to say.

Style: Writing and Reading as the Discovery of Outlook, by Richard M. Eastman (New York: Oxford University Press, 1978) is not a household word like Strunk & White or Flesch, but it is worth a look. It is a formal textbook, with lots of quoted examples and useful exercises; it is based on the "two complementary premises that style is outlook, and that outlook is discoverable through the act of writing itself" (p. ix).

A subcategory is books that tell you *how* to write, in the most basic sense: first you sit down, then you open your pen/put paper in your typewriter/turn on your word processor, then you make an outline . . . (As the sportswriter Red Smith put it, "Writing's easy. You just sit down at the typewriter and open a vein.") We are wary of recommending any of these, partly because they tend to be written at the fifth-grade reading level, partly because experienced writers differ so widely in their physical approaches. Some compose their first draft while weeding the bean patch or riding horseback; by the time they sit down in their studies, they need only transcribe what is already in their heads. Others jot down notes, which they keep beside them as they write. Some have to draft straight through, and until they get the beginning right they can't proceed; others write paragraphs as they think of things and add the beginning and end when they are arranging them in order. A bright young writer in search of advice is said to have asked S. J. Perelman how many drafts he went through. "Eighteen," the great man replied promptly. "At seventeen the writing is still rough; at nineteen I find it *recherché*."

But by all means, if you have trouble getting started, look through some of these books and see if any of them looks congenial. To quote Watkins' Law: "Articles which never get started never get finished."*

There is another subcategory of how-to-write books, written by genuine prose stylists. You may disagree with much of their specific advice, but in the course of disagreeing with a fine mind that has given much thought to the subject, you will clarify your own thoughts. (Some of the books we will mention are out of print—but the woods are full of good used-book finders, and for Fowler alone it is worth making the acquaintance of one.)

James Jackson Kilpatrick, in *The Writer's Art* (Kansas City: Andrews, McMeel, 1984), gives a lively account, always worth heeding, of the abuse our language has taken and what we can do to avoid battering it further. His alphabetical listing of disputed usages is engagingly titled "My Crotchets and Your Crotchets." Here is Kilpo on clarity: "If Saint Paul had been talking to a classroom of prospective writers, he might have changed a consonant. Faith and hope must abide, for the writer must have faith in his own ideas and he must hope that his words will be read,

---

*Alan Watkins, the distinguished British political correspondent.

but after faith and hope comes clarity. Without clarity we are not even sounding brass or tinkling cymbals. Be clear, be clear, be clear! Your idea or image may be murky, but do not write murkily about it. Be murky clearly!" (p. 32).

Style, by F. L. Lucas (London: Cassell, 1953), is first of all concerned with precision: "It seems that, within a few hours in the Crimea, first of all Lord Cardigan's misinterpreting of Lord Lucan's orders wasted the victory of the Heavy Brigade, and then Lord Lucan's misinterpreting of Lord Raglan's orders caused the suicide of the Light Brigade." But he continues: "[Style] involves, first of all, the power to put facts with clarity and brevity: but facts are usually none the worse for being put also with as much grace and interest as the subject permits" (pp. 16–17).

Herbert Read's *English Prose Style* (London: G. Bell and Sons, 1928) aims to distinguish between modes of expression appropriate to different sorts of writing. Some of his opinions strike us as bizarre—for example, that metaphor has no place in prose writing—but he is interesting on the effects of different sentence lengths and structures, and on the power of truly elevated prose: "Eloquence is, indeed, closely related to Glory, for one is the expression in deeds, as the other is in words, of the same animating principle of human conduct" (p. 201).

Arthur Quiller-Couch's *On the Art of Writing: Lectures Delivered in the University of Cambridge 1913-1914* (Cambridge: Cambridge University Press, 1923) is a period piece, but a charming one. There is nothing dated about his advice to make our writing "appropriate, perspicuous, accurate, and persuasive." Here is a sample of his own style in full flight: "I say that . . . 'antibody' is no word to throw at a friendly bacillus. . . . The man who eats peas with his knife can at least claim a historical throwback to the days when forks had but two prongs and the spoons had been removed with the soup. But 'antibody' has no such respectable derivation" (pp. 34–35).

Bonamy Dobrée, in *Modern Prose Style* (Oxford: Oxford

University Press, 1934), is concerned with changes in writing that reflect changes in society: "Prince Hal probably spoke fairly current English; and the journalists of the time, Nashe, Greene, Dekker, wrote much in the way Prince Hal spoke, for they were not labouring after fine style, but trying to write as men talked. What appears to have happened is that in the seventeenth century a profound division developed between the spoken and the written language, a division bridged by the journalists and the comic writers. What seems to have occurred afterwards was, to cut a long story short, that the journalists, forgetting Dryden, deserted to the written side: one has only to think of Addison, and then of Dr. Johnson, who, far from trying to write as he naturally spoke, did his best to model his conversation on his writing" (pp. 215–216).

Robert Graves & Alan Hodge, in *The Reader over Your Shoulder* (New York: Macmillan, 1944), begin with a lively account of the development and decline of English prose from the days of the Norman Conquest—"English is a vernacular of vernaculars"—to their own time: "It is not that modern people are less intelligent than their grandparents; only that, being busier, they are less careful. . . . People in important positions use a ragged conversational style that in the leisured Eighties would have been attributed to drink, mental decay or vicious upbringing." What would they have said, we wonder, about the style of our far less leisured Eighties?

DICTIONARIES

There are four major families of American dictionaries currently in print and available in most bookstores: Merriam-Webster, World, American Heritage, and Random House. Of course, as with other sorts of books, some of the best dictionaries are out of print. Remember the outcry when *Webster's Second* was replaced by *Webster's Third*? Here is an account which, with some fictional furbelows, reminds us that people who care about dictionaries at all care passionately:

> 'I'd better explain' [says Archie Goodwin]. 'Mr. Wolfe is in the middle of a fit. . . . He's seated in front of [the fireplace], on a chair too small for him, tearing sheets out of a book and burning them. The book is the new edition, the third edition, of *Webster's New International Dictionary, Unabridged,* published by the G. & C. Merriam Company of Springfield, Massachusetts. He considers it subversive because it threatens the integrity of the English language. In the past week he has given me a thousand examples of its crimes. He says it is a deliberate attempt to murder the—I beg your pardon. . . .'
>
> [Wolfe] rarely stands when a caller enters, and of course he didn't then, with the dictionary, the two-thirds of it that was left, on his lap. He dropped sheets on the fire, turned to look at her, and inquired, 'Do you use "infer" and "imply" interchangeably, Miss Blount?'
>
> She did fine. She said simply, 'No.'
>
> 'This book says you may. Pfui. I prefer not to interrupt this auto-da-fé.'*

Among our own favorite dictionaries is one that has been issued several times under different publishers' imprints; the copy sitting here is titled *Webster's Encyclopedic Dictionary: A Library of Essential Knowledge,* Franklin J. Meine, editor in chief (Chicago: Columbia Educational Books, 1943). It is superb at distinguishing shades of meaning of abstract words. For concrete nouns, it supplies telling details, memorably phrased. For example, "**Bear** . . . in stock-exchange slang, a person who does all he can to bring down the price of stock in order that he may buy cheap: opposed to a *bull*, who tries to raise the price that he may sell dear." (Clearly written a Securities Exchange Act ago.) Or, "**Cat** . . . A name applied to certain species of carnivorous quad-

---

*Rex Stout, *Gambit* (New York: Bantam, 1964), p. 2.

rupeds of the feline tribe, many varieties of which have long been tamed and kept in houses for catching mice, &c., and are proverbial for their stealthiness and cunning." Or, "**Macaroni** . . . A dough of fine wheaten flour made into a tubular or pipe form, a favorite food among the Italians . . ."

Another old friend is the *Funk & Wagnalls New Standard Dictionary of the English Language*, Isaac Funk, editor in chief (New York: Funk & Wagnalls; the original *New Standard* dates from 1913; our standby is the 1940 edition). Sidney Landau—in *Dictionaries: The Art & Craft of Lexicography*,* a brilliant work with which we often disagree—says of a later edition of the *F&W* that it was the only truly unabridged American dictionary in print other than Mr. Wolfe's hated *Webster's Third* (contrary to Random House's claim for its big dictionary). Here is a sample of the *F&W*'s leisurely, informative style: "**inanimate** . . . 1. Destitute of animal life; not sentient; as, *wood is inanimate*. 2. Hence, destitute of or greatly lacking in animation or activity; dull, lifeless. 3. Without life or consciousness; as, *an inanimate corpse*."

But even if one of these older gems proves to be your plate of macaroni, you will probably want a more current dictionary as well (we used to say: a dictionary that would tell you how to spell *carburetor*, but we are now told that carburetors are giving way to fuel injection, so there you are: no dictionary can stay current for long on the technical side). We mentioned that there are four major "families." Landau explains that dictionary-making is such a hair-raisingly expensive proposition that publishers need to get extra mileage out of their citation files and their staffs by producing more than one size—the principal ones being unabridged, college, desk, and pocket.

We can start by eliminating Random House. The new *Random House Webster's College Dictionary*, editor in chief Robert B. Costello (New York: Random House, 1991), illustrates the

---

*New York: Scribner's, 1984.

dangers of riding the Zeitgeist. It is a laughing-stock even in progressive circles for its attempts to speak to up-to-the-minute sensitivities.* But the previous generation of Random House dictionaries wasn't much better. It's hard to imagine what fate Nero Wolfe would have found condign for the original Random House "unabridged"—*The Random House Dictionary of the English Language*, Jess Stein, editor in chief (New York: Random House, 1966). It doesn't merely suggest that *infer* can mean *imply*, it actually uses the latter word as the third definition of the former; it meekly repeats every mistake anyone has ever made with *comprise*; it helpfully defines *inanimate* as "not animate."

The current *Random House* "unabridged" (1987, edited by Stuart Berg Flexner) compounds these errors with willfulness. To some of its disputed definitions it has added usage notes. These are well written in a combative style, but all the ones we've checked simply ratify the older *RH*'s attempts to do away with useful differentiations. Double pfui.

Next, in ascending order, come the American Heritage dictionaries. Their makers sought to benefit from the fuss over *Webster's Third* and the 1966 *Random House*, and recruited a "usage panel"; the panel's recommendations are printed after the definitions of various disputed words. Apart from the usage panel, the original *American Heritage Dictionary of the English Language*, William Morris, editor (New York: American Heritage & Houghton Mifflin, 1969), was best known for its thorough investigation of common Indo-European roots. According to Landau, this disappeared from a later edition, but we notice it is back in

---

*It was also the subject of a lawsuit by the Merriam-Webster people, on the grounds that its use of the words "Webster's" and "college" together, plus its cover design, was an attempt to poach on Merriam's territory. Merriam won; but it was generally conceded that the word "Webster's" alone would not have been grounds for a suit, even though the Merriam-Webster line is the only direct descendant of Noah Webster's dictionaries. In American usage, "Webster's" is practically synonymous with "dictionary"; its use on other publishers' dictionaries can be taken, according to one's level of suspiciousness, as a homage to the founder of American lexicography, or as an unearned appeal to authority.

the one currently in the bookstores (Houghton Mifflin, 1985). However, the definitions we have checked are not especially distinguished.

The World dictionaries are better. Indeed the 1959 edition—*Webster's New World Dictionary of the American Language*, general editors Joseph H. Friend and David B. Guralnik (Cleveland and New York: World Publishing)—has some personality to its definitions, e.g., "**cat** 1. A small, lithe, soft-furred animal, domesticated since ancient times and often kept as a pet or for killing mice." Later editions—the current one is the third college edition, Victoria Neufeldt, editor (Cleveland: Simon and Schuster, 1988)—retain many of these definitions but have added pompous notes on disputed words, e.g., "**infer** . . . 3b. to indicate indirectly: imply—in this sense, still sometimes regarded as a loose usage."

The current Merriam-Webster college dictionary is *Webster's Ninth New Collegiate Dictionary*, Frederick P. Mish, editor (Springfield, Mass.: G. & C. Merriam, 1983).* *MW9* is, according to Landau, the best medium-sized dictionary for scientific and technical terms. For matters such as syllable division, however, we prefer the older *Webster's New Collegiate Dictionary*, John P. Bethel, general editor (1959), an abridgment not of *Webster's Third* but of *Webster's Second*. *MW9*'s definitions, like those of all the Merriam-Websters, are as impersonal as possible, but clear. And they all—going back at least to *Webster's Second*—offer extremely useful differentiations of near synonyms, in separate listings after various important words.

We have mostly been considering the so-called college dictionaries, because that is the size that suits most people's needs best: college dictionaries are small enough to keep in an ordinary bookshelf or on the edge of your desk, but contain most of the

---

MW9 is, Landau explains, essentially an updating of *MW8* (Henry Bosley Woolf, editor in chief), but *MW8* was a thoroughgoing revision of *MW7* (Philip Babcock Gove, editor in chief). These are all abridgments of *Webster's Third*, of which Gove was editor in chief.

words you'll run across in a day. If you need a comprehensive American dictionary that includes postwar terms, then *Webster's Third* is it—*pace* Mr. Wolfe. However, if up-to-dateness isn't the point, the elegant old *Webster's Second*—*Webster's New International Dictionary of the English Language,* second edition, William Allan Neilson, editor in chief (1934)—can sometimes be tracked down by an energetic bookfinder; like its collegiate offshoot it is impersonal but clear, and gives good advice on levels of diction.

Finally there is, sui generis, the *OED,* formally *A New English Dictionary of the English Language,* James A. H. Murray, chief editor; Henry Bradley, W. A. Craigie, and C. T. Onions, editors (Oxford: Clarendon Press, 1882–1928).* It is the only comprehensive historical dictionary of the English language (a historical dictionary being one that chronicles the evolution of each word, whereas synchronic dictionaries, the more usual sort, tell what the word means now, with only occasional historical excursions). The *OED* became affordable—in both money and the space required to house it—with the publication, twenty years ago, of the *Compact OED* (formally *The Compact Edition of the Oxford English Dictionary*), photographically reduced so that each page contains four pages of the original. The *OED* is unlikely to be anyone's only dictionary. You can scarcely flip through ten volumes (in the full-size version) to pin down the exact word you want; and to read the compact version most people need the magnifying glass provided in the slipcase. Furthermore, the *OED* is of no help on American spellings and modern tendencies in compound words. But everyone who writes (or reads, for that matter) should be able to lay hands on a copy.

---

*As soon as the *OED* team had finished the original dictionary, they started work on a Supplement, which is included in later printings of the full dictionary. Then in the 1950s work began on an additional supplement, issued in four volumes from 1972 to 1986 (R. W. Burchfield, editor).

OTHER REFERENCE WORKS

This is not the place to examine encyclopedias, gazetteers, and so on. However, we should mention a handful of particularly useful literary reference works.

There are many specialized quotation books, but the two comprehensive ones are *Bartlett's Familiar Quotations*, originally compiled in 1855 by John Bartlett, and the *Oxford Dictionary of Quotations*, originally edited by Alice Mary Smyth in 1941. Both have gone through several editions; *Bartlett's* is currently in its 15th, edited by Emily Morison Beck (Boston: Little, Brown, 1980); the *ODQ* is in its third (Oxford: Oxford University Press, 1979). Since with each new edition some older quotations have to be dropped to make way for later ones, you often have to look in more than one edition to find what you want—yet another reason why bookshelf space seems to be a contracting universe. Suffice it to say that *Bartlett's* is better on American quotations, the *ODQ* on British ones (and also at giving the original of lines uttered in a foreign language).

Brewer's Dictionary of Phrase and Fable, by E. Cobham Brewer, is a treasure trove of information—from the cabalistic use of *abracadabra*, to the information, under **Bark**, that "Dogs in their wild state never bark, but howl, whine, and growl. Barking is an acquired habit," to a list of Patron Saints (did you know St. Clare is the patron saint of television?), to the origin, possibly on the American frontier, of the phrase *at the drop of a hat*. This work, first published in 1870 (London: Cassell), is in its 14th edition, edited by Ivor Evans (New York: HarperCollins, 1989).

Webster's Dictionary of Proper Names, compiled by Geoffrey Payton (Springfield, Mass.: G. & C. Merriam, 1970) is a useful and highly opinionated listing of all sorts of proper names. It gets a lot into each entry—e.g., "**Aase** The mother of PEER GYNT, whose death is an important episode in Ibsen's play and in Grieg's incidental music." or: "**Izvestia** (1917) Soviet Russian daily newspaper, representing the government viewpoint (see PRAVDA) and reproducing government documents at length. (Russian, 'news.')"

A Dictionary of Foreign Words and Phrases in Current English, by A. J. Bliss (New York: Dutton, 1966), is, as the title suggests, not a foreign-language dictionary, but a guide to foreign terms commonly used by people writing in English, from *filioque* to *marijuana*.

Finally, a word about thesauruses, such as *The New Roget's Thesaurus in Dictionary Form*, edited by Norman Lewis (New York: Putnam, 1964). These are designed for those it's-on-the-tip-of-my-tongue situations. For our part, we have never found in a thesaurus a word that our *Webster's Encyclopedic* or *Funk & Wagnalls* failed to yield, but many writers use the thesaurus very successfully. One caution: unless the writer knows for certain what the word he has found there means, he had better look it up in a proper dictionary. We suspect that careless use of the thesaurus is how the writer mentioned in Chapter Two came up with those wonderful bloopers.

Word Notes

O NE OF the great glories of the English language is the richness of its vocabulary, starting, as Robert Graves & Alan Hodge point out, with the importation of a whole second set of words (and therefore concepts) with the Norman Conquest. In the intervening centuries, English has gleefully picked up words from every culture it has come into contact with. (Quick: To whom do we owe *intelligentsia*? *yogurt*? *amuck*?) Meanwhile, as spelling was being codified, homonyms were sorted out and different spellings were applied to different sets of meanings.

This is to say that our modern spelling is not a matter of Natural Law, or even Grimm's Law. There is no easy mnemonic for most pairs of words that are easily confused, but we hope that listing a few of them will warn writers of their existence, and also give some clues to what other spellings to try if the dictionary doesn't seem to be yielding up the right word. (We have gleaned this list, we should mention, from the manuscript submissions of some highly literate but careless writers.)

Many of these words are extremely common—so common that most of us will have heard them (or at least heard one of the pair) before ever seeing them written. This is one source of confusion.

> **pore**, "to study intently," is of Anglo-Saxon origin and is not related etymologically either to **pour**, "to cause to flow" (of Welsh origin), or to **pore**, "a small opening in a solid body" (of Old French origin).

> **hale,** "sound and healthy," is of Anglo-Saxon descent and closely related to **hail,** meaning both "to greet" and, by long-established metaphorical extension, "to originate," as in, *He hails from Ohio*; but neither is related to **hail,** which damages your crops, or **hale,** "to haul" (which came through Old French), as in, *The bailiff haled him before the judge.*

> **horde,** "a tribe or great crew," comes to us from Turkish and Persian via French; **hoard,** "a cache of something valuable," with its verb meaning "to hide such a cache," is a native Anglo-Saxon word.

> **sew,** with needle and thread, is pronounced like **sow,** what you do with seeds, but unlike **sow,** "an adult female pig"; **sough,** "to make a noise like the wind," is prounced *suf.* All are of different Anglo-Saxon origins.

> **role,** "a part in a play," and **roll,** with a dozen meanings—from "a small bready item," to "to go around and around," to "a scroll on which medieval records were kept"—are both derived via French from the Latin *rotulus,* little wheel.

Concrete words can develop widely varying metaphorical extensions—as *cat* can mean a sharp-tongued woman or a sort of whip. But if a child or a foreigner called Fido "cat," you could produce a small, lithe member of the feline tribe, or its picture, to show what Fido is not. Abstract words can all be illustrated by examples, but the thing itself cannot be brought before the speaker, and so these words are more subject to misuse. We have mentioned some of these elsewhere (*comprise* and *compose; protagonist* and *proponent; masterful* and *masterly*); here are some more examples:

> **grisly,** meaning "horrible, frightful," derives from Anglo-Saxon; **grizzly,** the name of a large North American bear, derives from a French word meaning "greyish." "Grizzly" could easily have been spelt *grisly,* since its French ancestor has an *s*; but the common spelling mistake is the reverse: "the grizzly details." Neither is related to **gristly,** "containing gristle or cartilage."

> **principle,** "a general truth," and **principal,** "first or major,"

derive from related Latin words meaning "first in order."
Confusing the two is both a common error and one likely to
mislead; if the writer uses *principle* when he means *principal*,
the reader will be left wondering if perhaps he meant *principled*.

affect and **effect** come from related Latin words and sometimes intertwine. To *affect* something is to have an *effect* on it;
but to *effect* something is to bring it about.

A special subcategory is the group of words beginning in
for- and *fore-*. The *for-* prefix has a shifting negative sense—that is,
it intensifies negative stems and turns positive ones negative. The
fore- prefix refers almost exclusively to time and space, as in
be*fore*, but there are anomalies: preceding can acquire a negative
function—you might *go before* in order to **forestall**. (Compare the
non-negative use of *prevent* in "Lord, we pray thee that thy grace
may always prevent and follow us.") There are important cases in
which the same stem can take either *for-* or *fore-* with very different meanings:

forego means "to go before"; **forgo** means "to do without."
A *foregone* conclusion is one that was decided in advance, not
one that the participants decided to ignore.

forebear means "predecessor or ancestor"; **forbear** means
"to restrain oneself." You *forbear* to tell an antagonist what
you think of his *forebears*.

A frequently confused pair, though with different stems, is
foreword, "the preface to a book," and **forward**, the opposite of
backward.

Some other Pairs & Snares (Fowler's term) are:

envision, "to form a mental picture," and **envisage**, "to
face." Both words are quite new, compared to the oldtimers
we've been considering. *Envisage* is, as Fowler puts it, a
"19th-century word only, & a surely undesirable Gallicism";
the first use the *OED* gives of *envision* is by Lytton Strachey
in 1921. *Envisage* has, oddly, nearly supplanted *envision*—

oddly, because *envision* is so clearly related to its stem, *vision,* that there should be no grounds for confusion.

A. P. Herbert (who has an "entrance examination for words and phrases seeking admission to the English language") might pose another question: Do we need *envision* when we have *imagine*? "Need" may be going too far; but *envision* is sufficiently different in connotation to be useful—just as we have both *visionary* and *imaginary.*

fortuitous, "by happenstance," and **fortunate**, "lucky," both derive from a Latin word meaning chance, and there are many cases where both words apply. But there are *fortunate* events that are not *fortuitous,* and vice versa. And even where either might be used, the idioms differ: *He is very fortuitous to be alive* is not English, nor is *Their taking the same flight was purely fortunate.*

tortuous, "twisting, convoluted," is frequently confused with an adjective **torturous**, which if it were a recognized word (Who sez you can't?—though given the confusion we might do better to stick to "agonizing") would mean "causing severe anguish." Both derive ultimately from a Latin word meaning "to twist," but *tortuous* has no emotional connotation; *The road (or the senator's logic) was tortuous.*

winning has as a subsidiary meaning "attractive, pleasant"; **winsome**, from a different Anglo-Saxon root, means "causing joy or pleasure." A baseball pitcher may have a *winsome* manner, but he has a *winning* streak.

Finally, there are cases where Differentiation (Fowler's term) has taken place, so that two words, once used interchangeably, have had their meanings usefully divided up. Thus:

presently, "in due course," and **currently**, "going on now." This is a hard one to fight for—since *present* and *current* are virtual synonyms—but there are times when it is nice to have a simple -*ly* adverb to mean "in due course," and so we say: Fight on!

alternate, "in a pattern of first one, then the other"; **alternative**, "offering another possibility." The distinction is useful, although it has been undermined by the phrase, *take an alternate route.*

disinterested, "not having a stake in"; **uninterested,** "not taking an interest in." *Disinterested* is one of the words linguistic traditionalists will go to the mat for; latitudinarians, including most present-day dictionary-makers, point out loftily that it and *uninterested* were once synonyms. But since there is no other word that means "without regard to personal advantage" (as *Webster's Second* defines it), it is worth preserving the one we have.

REFERENCES

Chapter One

1. Whittaker Chambers, *Witness* (New York: Random House, 1952), p. 25.

2. Albert Jay Nock, *A Journey Into Rabelais's France* (New York: Grosset & Dunlap, 1934), p. 37.

3. Andrew Nelson Lytle, "A Myth in a Garden" (originally published in *Chronicles*, June 1987), in *From Eden to Babylon* (Washington: Regnery Gateway, 1990), p. 192.

4. Eudora Welty, *One Writer's Beginnings* (Cambridge: Harvard University Press, 1984), p. 3.

5. Flannery O'Connor, "The Barber," in *Complete Stories* (New York: Farrar, Straus, 1979), p. 15.

6. Richard M. Weaver, *Ideas Have Consequences* (Chicago: University of Chicago Press, 1948), p. 1.

7. Thornton Wilder, "Toward an American Language," in *American Characteristics and Other Essays* (New York: Harper & Row, 1979), p. 3.

8. Douglas Bush, "An Apologie for the Scepticall Reader," in *Engaged and Disengaged* (Cambridge: Harvard University Press, 1966), p. 11.

9. Karl Shapiro, *Essay on Rime* (New York: Reynal & Hitchcock, 1945), p. 7.

10. Forrest McDonald, *E Pluribus Unum: The Formation of the American Republic 1776–1790* (Indianapolis: Liberty Press, 1979), p. 27.

11. William Alexander Percy, *Lanterns on the Levee: Recollections of a Planter's Son* (Baton Rouge: Louisiana State University Press, 1977), p. 3.

12. David Cohn, *Where I Was Born and Raised* (South Bend: University of Notre Dame Press, 1967), p. 12.

13. Albert Jay Nock, "A Study in Manners," in *On Doing the Right Thing* (Freeport, N.Y.: Books for Libraries Press, 1971), p. 185.

14. *Mark Twain's Autobiography* (New York: Harper & Brothers, 1924), Vol. II, p. 92.

15. Ralph Waldo Emerson, "Self-Reliance," in *Essays, First Series* (Boston: Houghton Mifflin, 1896), pp. 50–51.

16. Herman Melville, *Moby Dick* as if you didn't know (New York: Random House, 1926), pp. 1–5.

17. James Russell Lowell, *Latest Literary Essays and Addresses: Old English Dramatists* (Boston: Houghton Mifflin, 1892), p. 91. Being Vol. XI of the Standard Library Edition.

18. José Ortega y Gasset, *El Tema de Nuestro Tiempo* (Madrid: Alianza Editorial, 1981), pp. 16–17. Translation: WFR.

19. Ortega y Gasset, *El Libro de las Misiones* (Madrid: Colección Austral, 1965), pp. 128–129. Translation: WFR.

20. Ortega y Gasset, *Origen y Epílogo de la Filosofía* (Madrid: Colección Austral, 1980), p. 89. Translation: WFR.

21. Nock, *Memoirs of a Superfluous Man* (Chicago: Henry Regnery, 1964), pp. 162–163.

Chapter Two

1. John McPhee, "Firewood" (originally published in *The New Yorker*, 1974), in *Pieces of the Frame* (New York: McGraw-Hill, 1975), p. 196.

2. S. L. Varnado, "The Gas Bill Also Rises," in *National Review*, March 31, 1978, Vol. XXX, p. 394.

3. Evelyn Waugh, *Scott-King's Modern Europe* (Boston: Little, Brown, 1949), pp. 10–11.

4. E. M. Forster, *Howards End* (New York: Vintage, 1921), pp. 49–50.

5. William F. Buckley, Jr., "The End of the Latin Mass" (1967), in *The Jeweler's Eye* (New York: Putnam, 1968), p. 322.

6. Kingsley Amis, *Lucky Jim* (New York: Viking, 1958), p. 64.

7. Forster, *op. cit.*, p. 31.

8. Sir Frederick Pollock and Frederic William Maitland, *The History of English Law Before the Time of Edward I*, second edition (Cambridge: Cambridge University Press, 1968), Vol. II, pp. 673–674.

9. Alexander Pope, *Essay on Criticism*, ll. 333–336.

10. *Ibid.*, l. 297.

11. *Fourth Year Latin*, edited by Lois Carlisle and Davida Richardson (Norwood, Mass.: Allyn and Bacon, 1933), p. 482.

12. C. S. Lewis, "*De Descriptione Temporum*" (1955), in *Selected Literary*

Essays, edited by Walter Hooper (Cambridge: Cambridge University Press, 1969), pp. 13–14.

13. Vladimir Nabokov, *Speak Memory: An Autobiography Revisited* (New York: Putnam, 1966), p. 12.

Chapter Three

1. Henry David Thoreau, *The Maine Woods* (New York: Norton, 1950), p. 291.

2. Nathaniel Hawthorne, *The Scarlet Letter* (New York: 1850; Random House Modern Library).

3. George Bancroft, *History of the United States,* 17th edition (Boston: Little, Brown, 1859), Vol. I, p. 39b.

4. John Maynard Keynes, *The Economic Consequences of the Peace* (1919), as republished in *Essays in Persuasion* (New York: Norton, 1963), p. 7.

5. William Alexander Percy, *Lanterns on the Levee* (New York: Knopf, 1941), p. 14.

6. M. J. Sobran, Jr., "The Newborn Garry Wills," in *National Review,* June 22, 1973, Vol. XXV, p. 681.

7. John Cheever, *Falconer* (New York: Ballantine, 1975), p. 171.

8. Richard M. Weaver, *The Ethics of Rhetoric* (Chicago: Henry Regnery Company, 1953), p. 144n.

9. William Shakespeare, *Richard the Second,* Act II, Scene 1. For what it's worth, let us note in this place that we are persuaded by the Ogburn arguments that the works attributed to the bumpkin "Shakspere" were from the hand of Edward de Vere.

10. Shakespeare, *Othello,* Act II, Scene 1.

11. Sir Philip Sidney, *The Defence of Poesy* (c. 1579), summary of first part.

12. Samuel Sewall, *Apocalyptica, or The New Heaven as it makes to Those upon the New Earth* (1697), as quoted in Ferris Greenslet, *The Lowells and Their Seven Worlds* (Boston: Houghton Mifflin, 1946), p. 23.

13. Paul Elmer More, "Criticism" (1910), in *Shelburne Essays* (New York: Phaeton, 1967), Vol. VII, p. 22.

14. T. S. Eliot, *The Idea of a Christian Society* (New York: Harcourt, Brace, 1940), p. 13.

15. Karl Shapiro, *Essay on Rime* (New York: Reynal & Hitchcock, 1945), p. 39 (line 1,061 ff.). This magnificent work, running some two thousand lines, is the best thing in the genre since Alexander Pope's *Essay on Criticism* (1709). Both are the work of youthful genius: Shapiro was thirty-one, Pope scarce twenty-one when they wrote these classics.

16. Conrad Aiken, "Tetelestai," in *A Little Treasury of Modern Poetry* (New York: Scribner's, 1952), p. 325. "Tetelestai" is usually translated "It is finished." It is New Testament Greek: cf. John 19:30.

17. Shakespeare, *Hamlet*, Act I, Scene 1.

18. Samuel Pepys, *Diary*, October 27, 1668.

19. Joan Didion, *Slouching Towards Bethlehem* (New York: Simon and Schuster, Touchstone paperback, 1979), p. 135.

20. Geoffrey Chaucer, *A Treatise on the Astrolabe*, in Chaucer's *Works* (London: Oxford University Press, 1912), p. 405.

21. Edward Hare, in Richard Hakluyt, *Principal Voyages, Traffics, and Discoveries of the English Nation* (London, 1598–1600).

22. Robert Burton, "Democritus Junior to the Reader," in *The Anatomy of Melancholy* (London, 1621).

23. Izaak Walton, *The Compleat Angler*, Chapter 4.

24. Charles Dickens, *Hard Times*, the ending. And good riddance!

25. Percy, in a letter to his father, LeRoy, October 25, 1918, as quoted in *The Percys of Mississippi*, by Lewis Baker (Baton Rouge: Louisiana State University Press, 1983), p. 86.

26. James Joyce, *Ulysses* (New York: Random House Modern Library, 1934), p. 641.

27. Tennessee Williams, in *The New York Times*, November 21, 1976.

28. Walter Ralegh, *A Report of the Truth of the Fight about the Açores This Last Summer Betwixt the Revenge, One of Her Majesty's Ships, and an Armada of the King of Spain* (London, 1591). Opening sentence. Title usually given in short form, *Narrative of the Revenge*.

29. John Milton, *Areopagitica* (London, 1644).

30. Samuel Johnson, *The Rambler*, No. 158, September 21, 1751.

31. Walter Bagehot, "The Reconstruction of the Union," in *The Economist*, September 16, 1865, Vol. XXIII, pp. 1,113–1,114.

32. Woodrow Wilson, *A History of the American People* (New York: Harper, 1903), Vol. III, p. 40.

Chapter Four

1. *The New York Times*, September 19, 1973.

2. Graham Chapman, John Cleese, Terry Gilliam, Eric Idle, Terry Jones, and Michael Palin, "The Dead Parrot," *Monty Python's Flying Circus*.

3. Edmond Rostand, *Cyrano de Bergerac*, ll. 315–358. Translation: LB.

4. Tom Wolfe, "Mau-Mauing the Flak Catchers" (1970), in *The Purple Decades: A Reader* (New York: Berkley Books, 1983), p. 202.

5. Wolfe, "These Radical Chic Evenings" (1970), in *The Purple Decades*, p. 182.

6. H. L. Mencken, "The Sahara of the Bozart" (1917), in *A Mencken Chrestomathy: His Own Selection of His Choicest Writings*, edited and annotated by HLM (New York: Knopf, 1949), pp. 185–186.

7. Mark Twain, *The Innocents Abroad*, Chapter XXVII.

8. Miguel de Cervantes, *Don Quixote de la Mancha*, translated by Peter Motteux (New York: Random House Modern Library, 1930), Part II, Chapter XLIII.

9. P. G. Wodehouse, *Right Ho, Jeeves* (New York: Penguin, 1953), p. 8.

10. Myles na Gopaleen, *The Best of Myles* (New York: Walker, 1968), p. 197.

11. *Ibid.*, p. 190.

12. Quoted by H. W. Fowler, *Modern English Usage* (Oxford: Clarendon Press, 1926), p. 349.

13. Willmoore Kendall, *The Conservative Affirmation in America* (Lake Bluff, Ill.: Regnery Gateway, 1985), p. 51.

14. Mark Twain, *A Connecticut Yankee in King Arthur's Court*, Chapter XXII.

15. W. H. Auden, "Precious Five," in *Collected Poems*, edited by Edward Mendelson (New York: Random House, 1991), p. 588.

16. Manning Coles, *The Man in the Green Hat* (New York: Carroll and Graf, 1986), p. 152.

17. Evelyn Waugh, *Brideshead Revisited: The Sacred and Profane Memories of Captain Charles Ryder* (Boston: Little, Brown, 1979), p. 9.

18. Auden, *The Dyer's Hand* (New York: Vintage, 1968), pp. 111–112.

19. Wodehouse, *The Clicking of Cuthbert and Other Stories* (Harmondsworth: Penguin, 1962), p. 12.

20. Wodehouse, *Right Ho, Jeeves*, p. 8.

21. Stan Kelly-Bootle, *The Devil's DP Dictionary* (New York: McGraw-Hill, 1981), pp. 128–129.

22. Dorothy L. Sayers, *Introductory Papers on Dante* (New York: Barnes & Noble, 1969), pp. 64–65.

Chapter Five

1. Thomas Paine, *The American Crisis*, opening sentences.

2. William Shakespeare, *The Merchant of Venice*, Act V, Scene 1.

3. Richard Brinsley Sheridan, *Clio's Protest*.

4. Charles Dickens, *A Tale of Two Cities*, opening sentence.

5. Edmond Rostand, *Cyrano de Bergerac*, ll. 2,534–2,541.

6. Willa Cather, *My Antonia*, last sentence.

7. Shakespeare, *Hamlet*, Act I, Scene 4.

8. Thomas Hobbes, *Leviathan*, Chapter 13.

9. Shakespeare, *Hamlet*, Act II, Scene 2.

10. *Ibid.*, Act IV, Scene 4.

11. John Masefield, "Sea Fever."

12. Genesis 2:23.

13. Shakespeare, *Julius Caesar*, Act III, Scene 2.

14. Abraham Lincoln, the Gettysburg Address.

15. Shakespeare, *Hamlet*, Act V, Scene 2.

16. John Milton, *Samson Agonistes*, ll. 98–104.

17. Genesis 9:1–2.

18. William Blake, "The Tyger."

19. Benjamin Franklin, remark to John Hancock on signing the Declaration of Independence, July 4, 1776.

20. Shakespeare, *Hamlet*, Act III, Scene 1.

21. William Wordsworth, sonnet "London, 1802."

22. I Corinthians 15:55.

23. Shakespeare, *Merchant of Venice*, Act III, Scene 1.

24. e. e. cummings, *Collected Poems* (New York: Harcourt, Brace, 1926), #297.

25. Acts 21:39.

26. Robert Burns, "Willie Brewed a Peck o' Maut."

27. John Keats, sonnet "On First Looking into Chapman's Homer."

28. Alexander Pope, *Essay on Criticism*, ll. 356–357.

29. Matthew 10:39.

30. Rudyard Kipling, "Danny Deever."

31. Burns, "John Anderson My Jo."

32. Pope, *op cit.*, ll. 388–389.

Following an exchange of letters with William F. Buckley Jr. on a point of grammar, Linda Bridges joined *National Review*'s editorial staff for the summer of 1969. She returned to *NR* in 1970, after completing her degree in French and English literature at USC. She became Managing Editor in 1988.

William F. Rickenbacker has been associated with *National Review* as writer, contributor, associate editor, or senior editor since 1960. He began linguistic studies early, majored in languages and literature at Harvard, and has pursued those studies, he says, like a terrier that smells a rat, since graduation in 1949. He has been anthologized in at least one college textbook on prose style.